H.O.P.E.
Hearing Other People's Experience
COLLEGE EDITION

Real Stories,
Real Students,
Real Audacity to

SUCCEED

DR. VERONIE LAWRENCE

Please send your comments about this book to DrVee@oneseedsolutions.com

Publisher Name: OneSeedSolutions LLC. Contact www.lchanelink.biz

Hearing Other People's Experiences (H.O.P.E.) College Edition; Real Stories, Real Students, Real Audacity to Succeed.

Copyright © 2021 by Veronie Lawrence, Ed.D., MDiv.

This title is also available on Amazon and BN.com as an E-book product.

Hearing Other People's Experience (H.O.P.E.) College Edition; Real Stories, Real Students, Real Audacity to Succeed may be purchased in large quantities for educational, business, or sales promotional use. For information email DrVee@oneseedsolutions.com

---

Library of Congress Control Number: 2021914255

Lawrence, Veronie.
Hearing Other People's Experiences (H.O.P.E.) College Edition; Real Stories, Real Students, Real Audacity to Succeed.

ISBN   (Print) 978-1-7375966-0-8
ISBN   (E-book)

All rights reserved. No part of this publication may be reproduced, stored in a retrieval system, or transmitted in any form or by any means-electronic, mechanical, photocopy, recording, or anyother-except for brief quotations in printed reviews, without prior permission of the publisher or author.

Edited by
Monica White, Ed.D.
Grand Pearl Communications, Inc.
www.gpcwrites.com
&
Jennifer Misick, Ph.D.

Cover Design & Content Layout
Tonya Thomas
Visual Solutions Unlimited
www.vsunlimited.com

Printed in the United States of America

Request for Dr. Veronie Lawrence to speak
One SEED Solutions, LLC
Email: DrVee@oneseedsolutions.com
Office: 1-833-SEEDS-01

DEDICATION

To my mother Gwendolyn C. Lawrence
To my Godmother Hermine M. White
To my Pastor, The Rev. Dr. J.G. McCann

You believed education was the key to bring forth change for self and others. Thank you for seeing what I could not and encouraging me to strive for greater.

Praise for Hearing Other People's Experiences, College Edition: Real Stories, Real Students, Real Audacity to Succeed

The multitude of issues facing our people while attending college are not often shared, yet these obstacles resonate with many college graduates. The H.O.P.E book is a well-documented collection of narratives that offers personal testimonies and life to the proverbial phrase, "If they can do it, so can I." Congrats to all those college degree recipients who stayed on the course despite the barriers.

–Dr. Ted N. Ingram, Professor, Bronx Community College,
Co-Author, *Engaging African American Males in Community College.*

This book allows the readers a window seat into the homes of college students that are living these everyday TRUTHS…keep speaking truth to POWER.

–Dr. Charise Breeden-Balaam, Food Insecurity Expert, Community College of Philadelphia, Visiting Lecturer, PA.

The H.O.P.E. College Edition is an engaging and essential resource, a primer for promising and current college students.

–Ms. Monique Fortune, MDiv, Adjunct Lecturer, Fordham University,
Author, *When Words Become Air, A Volume of Poetry*

HOPE, the college edition, provides us with powerful testimonies of college graduates that are a true reflection of what perseverance looks like when we create our own blueprint. While society would have us believe that our journey through higher education and life must follow one path, this work shows that there is no timeline in which a student must complete a degree. The only dreams that we cannot fulfill are those that we stop believing in. This book is a must-read not only for young people but, for adults that have stopped dreaming. Create and cross your own finish line.

–Kimberly C. Felder, Director of Corporate & Community Partnerships,
NYC Department of Education

And then there was H.O.P.E.--the students' stories in H.O.P.E. offer us a candid look at how to define strength and tenacity as driving forces for success. The lessons shared in each story are nuggets of wisdom that College students can embrace as valuable guides for taking the journey toward a degree and for those who are seeking strategic direction for maneuvering obstacles. I totally embraced the book as H.O.P.E offers an outstanding and solid read as a transformative tool for those on that journey toward that college degree.

–Betty J. Roberts, Ph.D. Retired Senior Higher Education Executive

Imagine if the wisdom of mentorship also came with a detailed blueprint. H.O.P.E not only documents the journey to success of recent college graduates, it also demystifies life's hard times by helping students understand that there are never any losses in life, only lessons. H.O.P.E delivers inspiration, a collection of sage advice, and a "how-to" guide to help you understand yourself, so you can unleash your greatest potential.

> –David Banks, President & CEO of The Eagle Academy Foundation
> Author, SOAR: *How Boys Learn Succeed and Develop Character*.

As an educator of more than 35 years, I have worked with countless students from various backgrounds, many with similar issues that Dr. Lawrence highlights in her phenomenal book. HOPE- is filled with rich experiences and tangible takeaways that would benefit any student who aspires to attend post-secondary students regardless of their station in life. This book is a need complication to add to the culture of academic success in higher education. Thank you, Dr. Lawrence.

> –Dorothy A. Escribano, Ph.D. Interim President/Provost Emerita
> The College of New Rochelle, NY

After reading this volume and lived experiences depicted, I was in awe of the authenticity. As Black, Indigenous, and People of Color (BIPOC), we have a host of obstacles to overcome and earning a college degree is vital to one's success. To all readers. Once you pick up this important work, your life will change for the better. H.O.P.E. College Edition is a must read!

> –Adreil A. Hilton, Ph.D. Vice Chancellor for Student Affairs &
> Enrollment Management
> Southern University at New Orleans.

H.O.P.E. College Edition is more than a compilation of stories, but a masterful weaving of the journey of overcomers! Each story has a nugget of inspiration and motivation for current and future college students. Open this book and be encouraged to make it to the finish line.

> –Stephanie S. Young, Ed.D., Educator and Consultant Educational Access
> Serving Youth (EASY) LLC, TN.

TABLE OF CONTENTS

Preface	1
Section 1 The Academic Roller Coaster	**3**
It's Not How You Start; It's How You Finish!	5
Don't Count Me Out: No Means Next Opportunity!	7
Do I Belong Here?	10
Knocked Down, but Not Knocked Out	12
Dr. Vee's SEEDs for Academic Success	15
Section 2 Financial Maze	**17**
The Balancing Act	18
The Gift of Life; In the Faces of Death	20
The Financing of Lights, Camera, Action!	22
Take the Limits Off	24
Dr. Vee's SEEDs for the Financial Maze	26
Section 3 Emotional Well-Being	**27**
Hey God, Where Are You?	28
Education beyond Our Borders; Dreams Do Come True	31
I Am More Than My Skin Color	34
Mind Over Matter	37
He Heard My Cry!	39
I Am Enough!	42
Dr. Vee's SEEDs for Emotional Well-Being	45
Section 4 Self-Discovery	**47**
Finding Self Through Education	49
The Village Beyond Home	52
The Crossover: Flame Out or Figure It Out	54
The Music Behind the Academics	57
Higher Education ABCs—Advocacy, Balance, and Communication	59
Dr. Vee's SEEDs for Self-Discovery	62

Section 5 Family Matters — 63
A Mother's Sacrifice — 65
There's No Place Like Home — 68
It's About the Right Fit! — 70
All in the Family — 73
And 5-6-7-8—It's The 8-count for me! — 76
Dr. Vee's SEEDs for the Family Matters — 79

Section 6 Non-Traditional Students — 81
The Breaks Did Not Break Me! — 83
Money Will Drive You, But Education Will Keep You — 85
It's a Different World — 88
Let's Get Clear! — 91
Reunited with My First Love Online — 94
Dr. Vee's SEEDs for the Non-Traditional Student — 97

Section 7 Building Blocks of Academic Success Skills — 99
Academic Success Skills — 100
Cornell Note Taking Method — 103
SQ3R Method — 104
Reading Strategies — 105
Time Management — 106
Time Management Self-Assessment — 107
Quick Tip: How to break down your semester — 108
Study Strategies — 109
Understanding your Study Cycle — 110
Test Taking and Study Strategies Self-Assessment — 111
Test Taking — 112
Test Taking Tips for Different Exam Questions — 113
Information Literacy — 116
Learning Styles — 117
Critical Thinking — 119
Emotional Well-being — 122
Financial Literacy — 125

PREFACE

The goal of any college aspirant is graduation! According to the National Center for Education Statistics (NCES), a federal entity collects, analyzes, and reports data related to education in the United States and other nations. The national average of completion of post-secondary studies is six (6) years. During this time frame students encounter life issues, greater self-awareness, persistence, critical thinking, and so much more. It is assumed these foundational characteristics serve a lifetime.

After two decades of teaching in various higher educational settings, including advising, counseling, and coaching countless students through their academic endeavors, I have reflected on my professional experiences and education journey and realize that I and many committed faculty members and administrators have often dealt with students who struggle with issues that include fitting in and adapting to new academic and social college norms. Our adeptness to support students in balancing their personal and academic lives wildly affects their academic achievement and attainment. A segment of the college process often overlooked is the life challenges that impact the college experience and possible degree completion. Often students are told they must wait to enroll to comprehend the intricate turns that await them during a college experience. Well, wait no longer. This installment in the H.O.P.E. series provides a glimpse into student self-efficacy and a commitment to graduation over 25 years. Each story is personal and uniquely expresses a persistence that the tassel is worth the hassle!

For years, the art of storytelling has been a way in many cultures to pass down history, experiences, and fortitude to those who will listen. H.O.P.E.—The College Edition provides an outlet and brings real-life experiences, advice, and lessons while giving a lifeline to students who are embarking on their college experience. These stories will inspire students to keep pushing, to have the audacity to succeed despite circumstances, and recognize that they are not alone in their experiences. By sharing other's experiences in the college journey, it becomes abundantly clear that you are not alone. An emotional connection is formed when students hear how other people have experienced a few bumps in their journey yet still managed to graduate. This gives HOPE and provides light to what is often an uncertain path in college. Years of anecdotal conversations coupled with quasi-explanatory research through real-life interviews provided the backdrop of the emotional context to the educational journey captured in this series.

Through my personal and professional experiences, I have found that self-efficacy is an essential variable to achieving the college education dream and relevant academic success skills. Skills that become building blocks for academic tenacity and levels the playing field. Skills that must be reinforced in and out of the classroom and offer a roadmap through challenging times. This installment in the H.O.P.E. series is more than a collection of stories. It is a unique complementary resource that should be included in the academic success toolkit for any student commencing or continuing their college journey. This must-read collection of stories highlights students' college experiences on their journey to college graduation from the early 2000s to the present. The stories and academic success skills presented as an appendix provide a holistic framework that adds to higher education culture.

Although my time as a first-year college student was some time ago, the skills I learned have supported my educational journey throughout my post-secondary studies. If I can survive my college experience, from having to sit out a semester, care for an ill parent, transfer to another school near the end of my journey, and lose college credits, then so can you. This book aims to inspire you and to plant a SEED: Support, Education, Empowerment, and Development.

This book is for you, the student, to understand that negative experiences do not define you. You, through your experiences, both negative and positive, are writing your unique journey. I hope the pages in this book motivate you to stay the course if you encounter a detour. Know that detours are not meant to derail you but to redirect your path. Let these experiences allow you to become laser-focused on achieving your goal. You, students, give us hope for a better tomorrow. Our responsibility is to provide you with the tools you need to be the best version of yourselves for tomorrow. This book can be a guide for you to achieve success.

"The only source of knowledge is an experience."—Albert Einstein

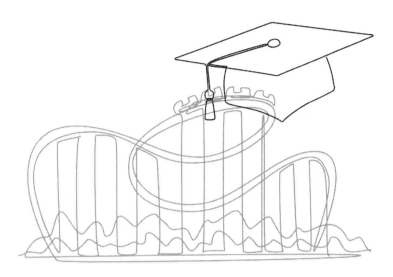

SECTION 1

THE ACADEMIC ROLLER COASTER

Get Ready! College has a new level of expectation waiting for you. The academic rules have changed since high school. Your success or failure of this leg of the academic journey lies solely with you, the student.

Academic highs and lows are part of the college journey. How you handle it will determine the level of success you will have in achieving your goal of obtaining a college degree. There are several factors to academic success that are both inside and outside of the classroom. For example, many students may experience their first low grade. Oh, the stress! Also true, though, a failing grade does not have to completely derail you. Many students move beyond these obstacles; it does not stop them. In fact, an overwhelming majority enroll the following semester repeating the course or charting a new plan of action for success.

You need to remember in difficult academic situations that you can recover from it. Failure is not a denial. Even if your journey is prolonged and your reward is delayed, you can still be successful. The academic roller coaster will challenge you to dig deeper, explore untapped resources, develop good study habits, create a schedule, and be prepared to explore new areas of study.

Academic success requires you to adjust from being in a formal high school classroom setting with small class sizes and peers who have been your classmates for a while to college and university lecture halls. Some have over 250 people enrolled in the class. Additionally, you may deal with the new awakening of not always being noticed as the brightest in the room. You instead blend in with the masses of other brilliant minds and have to adjust from being told what to do to be an active part of the learning dialog.

The academic challenges you may encounter during your college journey are varied and have serious consequences. For example, losing college credits leads to losing time and ultimately losing money! Whatever may come, just know that a shift in your thinking will be necessary. The goal is to learn how to ride this new academic wave until you find your balance.

The Academic roller coaster section highlights stories where students have encountered some of the challenges I've mentioned here and others. But, more importantly, the stories highlight the ultimate triumph over these challenges that determined students like you can make.

Enjoy!

IT'S NOT HOW YOU START; IT'S HOW YOU FINISH!

In 2010 I decided to attend Bronx Community College. Bronx Community College was not my ideal choice. My guardian at the time, which was my aunt, felt it was the best decision. She thought I wasn't ready to go away and become responsible for myself. I really think she wasn't ready to let me go. During my first semester at Bronx Community College, I was placed in the Learning Community program. I wasn't pleased about this as I wasn't able to earn many college credits; a part of me felt I was wasting my time. However, my advisor informed me that this program was set up for freshmen who needed to take two remedial classes to strengthen their skills in those areas. My schedule included Math 01 and English 02, freshman orientation, and Psychology 11, which was my only credited class. One of the benefits, though, was that I wasn't alone because I moved with a block of fellow students, which helped me get even more support. The program provided additional support from our professor's work in a collaborative manner.

I overcame many challenges, such as having to repeat remedial classes three times. I was so disappointed in myself for the time and money I felt was wasted. Also, I had to find a place to live, and it was no easy task, especially when one's finances were challenged. My journey was a little longer than most, I started in 2010, and I graduated in 2017. My focus shifted, I began working a second job and was excited to get my first apartment, so I put college on the back burner. I got caught up in life and friends, many of which had children, and dropped out of college too. So, it did not appear to be a concern for me or my circle. To my surprise, one day, I received a text from my mentor Dr. Ingram who was my freshman orientation professor. The same level of concern he showed when I was in his class was exhibited in this communication. He was clear, "get your butt back in school. You only need five classes to graduate." The text was just in time for registration, and I enrolled as a part-time student. Once I was back in the groove, it was such an eye-opener. Everything was different; I felt so out of touch. Professors who had supported me were gone; buildings changed, and there seemed to be a shift on the campus. So much had changed, but so had I. I used the changes as an opportunity to motivate myself—to get my life together, no more kidding around as I did previously.

My aunt was right! Community College was the right place for me. My professors cared and were always willing to offer support with any obstacles. In addition to graduating from Bronx Community College, my personal goal was to be on the Dean's list. I achieved this in my senior year and graduated with a 3.4 GPA. This was a major accomplishment because there was a time my transcript was full of C's and D's. My English classes bolstered not only my grades as I received A's, but this also helped my emotional state too. I decided then I would major in English at Lehman College.

When I graduated from Bronx Community College, I was relieved to finally be done with community college. But when I graduated from Lehman College, I felt accomplished. I felt successful and ready to start a career with the proper credentials to support me. Three months after graduating with my bachelor of arts degree in English literature, I was employed as a teacher assistant in a charter school located in Bronx, NY. In this role, I educated young scholars in the second grade. I know from personal experience that the road may be long for them, but they can finish as I did.

What is the greatest lesson learned?
Life is a marathon, not a sprint. You should not feel pressured to finish in a specific time frame.

What advice would you share with first year college student?
It's not how you start; it's how you finish. Seek the support. It is available to you. Don't give up.

D. Roundtree
Lehman College-CUNY | Class of 2019
Bronx Community College-CUNY | Class 2017

DON'T COUNT ME OUT.
NO MEANS NEXT OPPORTUNITY!

It's Harlem, baby! From uptown to down south is the pilgrimage of my college experience. My college exposure began at Thurgood Marshall Academy High School for Learning and Social Change, probably in the eleventh grade. The net was cast wide and included all college types, but there was a concerted push for Historically Black Colleges and Universities (HBCU) and Predominantly White Institutions (PWI). My college list consisted of both types of schools, about 50-50. So, let me just be honest! I knew college was the next step, but college wasn't that important at the time. I did what my guidance counselors told me. So, enrolling in Elizabeth City State University (ECSU) rested squarely on the shoulders of a recent graduate from my high school who returned home from ECSU. He had applications in hand and basically told a group of us, "I got you," so I submitted an application. I was one of approximately thirty (30) students to submit an application.

Twenty-five (25) students were accepted, and three of us enrolled in the fall 2009 semester. I felt good. I was now heading off to college with friends, but, in hindsight, that may not have been the best thing.

Since I was from Harlem, the transition to college was not difficult. I had attended a predominantly African American and Hispanic high school. So, it made enrolling and adjusting in an HBCU that much easier. The cultural and social assimilation was seamless, but adjusting to the academic rigor was a totally different story. Being a part of a graduating class of a little less than 100 people to a new community of more than 4000 people was exciting and nerve-racking all at the same time. The freedom, the responsibilities, and the adjustments all shared in the cultivation of my educational experience. The HBCU education experience catered to students like me; the professors provided students the tools needed to succeed during and after college. These newly acquired skills helped me understand how to navigate the world as a young black professional male in a world that often does not see us.

My college experience was further enhanced when I pledged Omega Psi Phi Fraternity, Incorporated, the Lambda Gamma chapter, in Spring 2011. I had gained 16 new brothers, and I was number five of the group.

The experience was life-changing in more ways than I can count. It was my first exposure to an organizational setting, mentorship, and accountability.

Unfortunately, until I learned better, I focused more on social and extracurricular activities. I joined Student Activities Committees (SAC). I also served as an Ambassador, which allowed me to attend football and basketball games to show school spirit. I also served in the Student Government Association (SGA) and the campus Panhellenic Council, fostering campus engagement. Helping incoming students find a way to make ECSU home was my specialty.

If I had put the same energy into my academic study as I did social engagement, I would have made the Deans' List every semester. Instead, I ended up with academic problems that could have derailed me permanently.

Better late than never, I eventually got focused. I had to pay the price and register for an overload of classes in my last two semesters. This is where my social contacts and networking played a valuable role. I participated in the athletic study hall, restructured priorities, and restricted all social activities. I can honestly say that without the guidance of the men of my fraternity, I would not have graduated. Yes, it took me five years to get to the point where I might be able to graduate from college; however, that time frame was about to be in jeopardy too. I was on academic probation for a year. I had to maintain a certain grade point average (GPA) or be dismissed from school. The partying, the social aspect of college life, had finally caught up with me. I now had another opportunity to correct bad habits and focus on the principles of what college and fraternity life is all about - being an exceptional student and leader.

To make a long story short, I was in the home stretch, and, a week before graduation, I discovered that I was missing an English class I needed to graduate. The panic that consumed me was overwhelming. This was compounded by the fact that the department head had counted me out for the 2014 graduation. I can still hear her words today "you are not going to graduate this semester." Furthermore, I had already pushed the limits on what financial aid would pay because of the number of failed classes and academic probation for one year. I felt defeated. However, a fraternity brother and now mentor's words overshadowed what I just heard. He said, "don't take no as the final answer." I was encouraged to seek out someone, anyone, who could help remedy the dilemma in which I found myself. I finally sought assistance from the Academic Affairs- College Level Examination Program (CLEP).

The advisor looked skeptically at me and my situation, handed me a booklet, and said, "You have 24 hours to study. Be back here at 8 a.m." While others were celebrating and getting ready for graduation, I was still studying. I studied all night long. The following day, I took the English test and PASSED! Graduation had almost eluded me! If it had not been for the mentoring and networking with faculty and staff on campus, I would not have made it.

The lessons learned, the undergraduate degree I earned, and my graduate degree will carry me throughout life. I am proud of who I have become because of those lessons. Through it all, I am proud to say that I graduated with a bachelor's degree in criminal justice. I'm also on track to earn a master of science degree in cybersecurity risk & strategy from New York University in the 2021 graduating class.

What is the greatest lesson learned?
I learned perseverance and that "No" doesn't always mean NO! It can simply mean you are knocking on the wrong doors. Also, do not let your mistakes define you. Lean into the lessons, not the mistake! Be open and honest about reaching for help in all areas - academically and emotionally. Take advantage of the wellness center services.

What advice would you share with first year college student?
Understand that adulthood begins when you decide to attend college. The decisions you make and the things you choose to experience are a microcosm of what your life will be like upon graduation. Begin to build your life while in college; don't wait until you have graduated. You will just have to work harder. Lastly, remember the 12-P's: Piss Poor Preparation Promotes Piss Poor Performance, Piss Poor Performance Promotes Pain!

Lamar Thornton
Elizabeth City State University | Class of 2014

DO I BELONG HERE?

I hail from Milwaukee, WI. Some may say I lived a sheltered life. I say I lived a life of love based on Christian principles and what my parents could afford. We were the typical blue-collar family making ends meet, and we lived in one of the most segregated places in the country. I attended King High School, located in Milwaukee. I was an above-average student, focused on college but no clear path to getting there. I entered college with a semester's worth of college credits as I had taken quite a few Advanced Placement (AP) classes in high school. In fall 1999, I enrolled in "Rattler Nation," Florida Agricultural and Mechanical University (FAMU).

I did not know I was about to learn in more ways than one, personally and academically. I had heard about HBCUs, but this was my first time being around so many affluent people of color. It was astonishing and overwhelming, but secretly I beamed with pride. I was surrounded by people whose parents were part of the Who's Who list, or CEOs, government officials, and were from the likes of Baldwin Hills. Their children were legacies of FAMU, sororities, and fraternities. It was a lot to take in. To my surprise, it took a toll on my self-esteem and affected how I felt about myself. I was nervous about speaking up in class; I had anxiety about going to class. I was fearful of being judged, being wrong, and I self-isolated. All of this was compounded with a personal relationship that was spiraling. I was insecure in the relationship; I thought we were in love and would enjoy our college years together-that was the furthest from the truth. This culminated with a 1.7 GPA and self-medicating with drinking. Needless to say, my parents were not pleased.

I was constantly in conversation in my head. Often it was not the most positive conversation. Still, a question kept replaying "do I belong here?" and for the first year or two, I was unable to answer the question in the affirmative. A phrase unfamiliar to me then, but as I reflect on my college experience, I realized I suffered from imposter syndrome. I constantly doubted my abilities and felt like a fraud. How could that be? How could I feel like an outcast at an HBCU? The internal conversation did not match up with my actual experience. Returning home without a degree was not an option. So, I sought out opportunities to fit it and express myself, I joined the FAMU newspaper, the theater club, and in my junior year, I was honored to accept membership into sensational Sigma Gamma Rho Sorority, Inc., Alpha Epsilon chapter in the Fall of 2001.

The isolation, the sense of feeling lost dissipated as I had found a sisterhood, support, and community.

In addition to the sisterhood, I had experienced a spiritual awakening. I was a Bethel Missionary Baptist Church member in Tallahassee, FL, and I had decided to read the entire bible in a year. I began to see myself as God saw me: we all come from a royal lineage. Owning that gave me more self-confidence to be who I am and express myself more openly. All of these experiences helped me to grow. I had to define myself for myself, not based on others' expectations. The self-discovery about myself during college was only the beginning, and it was priceless. I learned to trust myself in the simplest of things, such as knowing what study techniques worked best for me. For example, doing what others did not work for me. So, I had to lock myself in Lee Hall. I remember it clearly. I would study for hours. I studied for knowledge, not just to do the assignments. This process brought me full circle back to my AP style of academics and prepared me for graduation and law school. In 2004, after five (5) years, including summer school, my parents and I were ecstatic that I graduated with a bachelor of science degree in business administration with a 2.8 GPA. The exploration of self continued while I earned my master's degree in business administration in 2015. I was better prepared to enroll in Law school in 2020.

What is the greatest lesson learned?
It does not matter who you are or where you come from; everyone has value to bring to any situation. You can go as far as your motivation will take you.

What advice would you share with first year college student?
No matter how you feel, trust that someone else feels the same and you're not alone. Seek support.

Paula Hull
Florida Agricultural & Mechanical University | Class of 2004

KNOCKED DOWN, BUT NOT KNOCKED OUT

I was so eager to go to college! I had quite a few choices being a relatively good high school student-athlete (track and field). My eagerness to attend college and live on campus was fueled by the various campus visits I had experienced. I also had a strong desire to gain independence and leave my old-school West Indian mother's controlling grasp. However, I was conflicted. I had only arrived in the USA a few years before preparing to attend college. Even though I wanted to go out of state, I was afraid to go too far because I had not learned the USA nor New York. My plan was to go far enough that my mother had to call before coming but close enough that I could get home within a few hours and with minimal expense in case of an emergency. How I ended up at the first Historic Black College and University (HBCU)—Cheyney University is fuzzy. But, I did know someone from high school who was also attending, so that help helped.

I did not do well on the math section of my Scholastic Aptitude Test (SAT) So, I had to attend a pre-college program, ACT 101, which allowed me to strengthen my math skills and be ready for college in the fall. While in the program, I was training for the NYS Empire State Games and the track coach noticed me. The next thing I knew, I was on a partial track & field scholarship.

The fun, the friends, the fellowship that I experienced during my time in ACT 101 was, let's just say, too memorable to put into words. I had so much fun! While enjoying the beginning of young adulthood, I did not realize the level of anger that lurked inside of me. I did not realize how angry I was about certain events that transpired in my life. That anger erupted on the last day of ACT 101.

I got into a fight! Let's just say I am nice with my hands. There was a two-three week break between the end of ACT101 and the beginning of the fall semester. I went home to regroup and retrieve the remaining items I would need to start my college journey full-time. On the day I was returning, the car was all packed. I checked my mail, and there was a letter from the Cheyney University informing me I had been suspended for the 1990-91 academic year. WHAT! Oh Lord, this must be a mistake. I said nothing to no one. We headed down 95 South, and I plotted how I would resolve this problem without my mother losing her mind.

I arrived on campus, found my coach because we had to figure something out. He fought hard on my behalf, but the decision remained. I was scared! This new life that I had waited for was being placed on hold. I returned home to New York and stayed with a family member because I still needed my mother to think I was in school while I figured out my next move. I now know that was not the right thing to do, but it was what I came up with at the time. I kept up the charade until right before Thanksgiving. That's when my mother figured out I was not in school, but she still did not know the reason why.

I returned home; she was more relieved to see me than angry with me. I told her all that had transpired. Oh, my mother was not having it. She may not have had a college education, but no one was going to stop her daughter from obtaining what she had immigrated to the USA to do. My mother jumped into action and contacted her boss. My mother's employer, an attorney, swiftly had me reinstated within a matter of days. Apparently, there were some discriminatory practices as all parties had not been handled the same. I lost a whole semester out of fear. I returned more ready than ever to resume my studies and training in the fall of 1991.

My mother made me take a full academic load in summer school to make up for the semester I had missed out on acting like Mike Tyson's sister. I was back on track and back at Cheyney. I really enjoyed my time at Cheyney University, so it devastated me to make the difficult decision to leave a year later. The financial responsibilities, even with scholarships, work-study, etc., became too much. I was ahead of the scheduled graduation time frame and was on track to complete my studies in about three to three and half years. I just could not fathom taking out that much money in student loans. An added weight to my decision was that my mothers' health started to decline.

I needed to be closer to home. I was all she had. Heartbroken, I reluctantly returned to New York yet again. I transferred to The City University of New York (CUNY)-Hunter College and received another knockdown punch! I lost 21 credits in the transfer. All that work to be ahead of the game, lost! I was beyond angry, but I knew I could not remain in that space. I had become accustomed to certain things while at Cheyney, the likes of living away from home, on and off-campus, returning to my mother's home was not an option. I was relieved when I was accepted to Hunter College dorms, located on 23rd street, downtown NYC. The experience of city life was exciting and made up for being back home. It was great, but it was not the HBCU life I had grown to love and become used to.

I focused on my studies, participated in track and field for a semester, made some life-long friends, but I had tunnel vision for graduation. I wanted this chapter to be over and move to the next, even though I did not know what the next entailed. As focused as I was, my mother was equally as focused. She was clear she had not sent me to college to get into foolishness, and she was expecting to see someone, and that someone had better be me, graduating in four years.

Even after losing two semesters of education, being suspended from college, and transferring, I still managed to graduate meeting my mothers' wishes. Thank God for a winter commencement. I completed my studies in fall 1994 and graduated in 1995 with a bachelor of science degree in accounting. As a life-long learner, I have gone on to earn four more degrees.

What is the greatest lesson learned?
Don't let fear be your decision-maker. One obstacle or one punch may knock you down, but that does not mean you're out for the count. Get up, reassess, reinvent, and move forward.

What advice would you share with first year college student?
Success in college means you must learn how to manage multiple situations simultaneously. Set goals, manage your college experience, and don't let it manage you. Remember I AM—Intentionally take Action to Manifest your results.

Veronie "Dr. Vee" Lawrence, Ed.D.
CUNY-Hunter College | Class of 1995

DR. VEE'S SEEDS FOR ACADEMIC SUCCESS

These stories show the remarkable drive that each student made when faced with the highs and lows of the academic roller coaster. That drive is fueled by academic tenacity, which is an internal mindset that produces positive external results in academic performance, commitment, and sticktoitiveness. Academic tenacity is not about being the smartest, it is not giving up in the academic arena when the odds are stacked against you. Although academic tenacity can be elusive at times, all college students, including you, will benefit immensely when it is practiced early in the journey to assure their success.

Here are some things to consider for a wonderful ride and ultimate success. Just like any roller coaster, you may be in for a wild ride with a range of emotions from gleeful joy to fear. Still, the overall experience is a great one.

You can learn a lot from other roller coasters you've encountered in life. For instance, when you get ready to ride a roller coaster, you know what you are getting into and you do what is required for a successful ride: Follow all rules, ask questions if you don't understand or suspect something may be wrong, and ensure that your safety restraints are on and secure. This preparation is also apropos for the academic journey.

So, here are a few tips to help you on your academic ride. Be prepared each semester and seek support from professors, advisors. Also, know that midterms and final exam times can be rocky. You may scream or want to pull your hair out, or maybe you feel like your world is going to fall out from underneath you similar to a rollercoaster. However, if you stay the course, the end results in academic achievement and the lasting friendships make the academic roller coaster worthwhile, so hold on and smile!

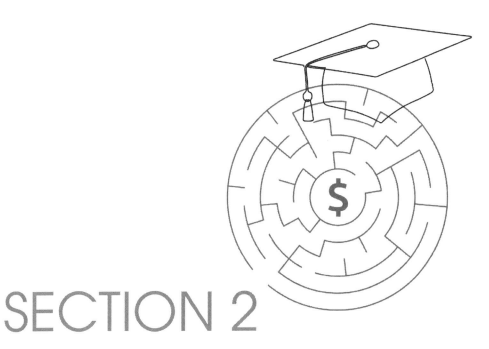

SECTION 2

FINANCIAL MAZE

The stories in this section show how to navigate the financial maze of the college experience. In a time when the cost of education has risen 10-fold, financial issues can be a central part of the problems related to attending college. The phenom social media mantra-like song, *"Where the Money Reside,"* is more than a catchy song lyric. It is at the core of what families, students, and colleges ask as students move through their academic journey. The lack of finances or money management is the primary reason why college students' journeys are unfortunately disrupted, delayed, or sometimes denied. However, this does not have to be the outcome.

Financial literacy can go a long way to ensuring you complete the college degree. This includes knowing when to apply for Free Application for Federal Student Aid (FAFSA), finding scholarships, and understanding a FREE credit card is not FREE.

These stories highlight the financial hurdles and breakthroughs students overcame to persist in their college dream of graduation.

THE BALANCING ACT

I had a plan, and I had to find the time and money to execute the plan. My plan was not an option; I had a pair of little eyes watching every move I made. So being intentional was key. The CUNY-Bronx Community College (BCC) life was the closest thing I could have asked for based on affordability and location. I had responsibilities outside of tuition so going away to college was not an option. The diversity of ages, ethnicity, and station of life made me comfortable; the transition was seamless based on my own life experience. I was a father and worked as a General Manager at McDonald's.

I enrolled in BCC Fall 2013 at the age of 25, ready for the next chapter of my life. The proximity to my residence was a bonus, so getting to and from school would not be an issue. Moreover, it would not require a financial strain since I could walk to campus, even during inclement weather. Proximity was also crucial since I was responsible for picking my son up after school. Even before enrolling at BCC, I would often frequent the campus, get my bearings, take in the campus life. It was difficult to believe this beautiful campus was the jewel in the middle of the hood. Every time I stepped foot on campus, I felt like I had been transported to a suburban town. This made studying and remaining on campus long after classes had ended pleasurable. I would bring my son to college with me. He would do his homework while I met with tutors or attended meetings.

I had worked as a manager running someone else's business for almost seven years, so I was clear about the area of study I wanted—Business Administration. My goal was to own my own business. I had hands-on experience, but I knew I needed the scholarly application. The balancing act of this new chapter of my life was not going to be easy, with fatherhood and school, and I wanted to be involved on campus. This was the only way I would truly get all I needed out of the college experience. The plan and the structure of ASAP—The Accelerated Study in Associate Program—was a lifesaver in more ways than one. My financial responsibility for school was reduced as they provided textbooks and MetroCards. This allowed my paycheck to go just a little further for my son and me. The built-in support of tutoring and the cohort model, where students travel through the academic program together, reminded me I was not alone on this journey. I sought community and found it ASAP. I also wanted the support of Black men, and I found a community in the Black Male Initiative under the leadership of Dr. Ingram and Dr. Knox. They further mentored me throughout my college experience. The experience in this initiative boosted my confidence, and it propelled me to run for Vice President and President of the Student Government Association. While in these positions, my goal was to learn how to take care of the needs of a small constituency, my BCC family, to eventually impact a larger constituency. I felt like I had put too much on my plate, but this was all part of my plan. I planned to major in Business Administration and use my knowledge of business and politics to empower black and brown people to use the power of voice, vote, and economic spending.

I eventually had to slow down just a little. My fatherhood responsibilities shifted drastically during my last year. I went from only having my son 50% to 100% of the time. My balancing act faulted; I received mostly Ds' that semester. I was able to bounce back and graduate with an Associate of Science in Business Administration and transfer to CCNY in the Fall of 2015. Another minor pause on the road to completion, but I'll be back to finish what I started. At the age of 10, my son still inquires about his first college experience at BCC. His eyes are still watching and looking out for the next degree.

What is the greatest lesson learned?
The world is not as simple as it seems. There is always room to grow.

What advice would you share with first year college student?
Don't give up! If you have a goal in mind, make a plan for that goal and keep pressing.

Q.P.
CUNY- Bronx Community College | Class of 2015

THE GIFT OF LIFE IN THE FACES OF DEATH

Very early on, I realized that I loved learning, and subsequently, I really liked school because I was good at it. I graduated from high school, number nine in my class, with decent test scores. Pretty impressive, right? Wrong. Much like many others, college's financial woes plagued me, I still struggled to pay for college. I attended the illustrious Hampton University in Hampton, VA. Hampton is a private historically black university (HBCU); therefore, it is expensive. My freshman year there was fully covered by financial aid and a few small scholarships. I made okay grades that year but definitely went into shock when I earned my first "C." I literally cried my eyes out. I had always been at the top of my class, or at least very close to it. However, after getting that grade, my confidence took a major hit, and so did my work ethic. I began to wonder, "Why am I working so hard if I'm only going to make C's?" After taking some time to reflect, I realized I did well for so long because I enjoyed school; I enjoyed learning. During sophomore year, I redeemed myself and brought my grade point average (GPA) back up. That is the definite truth about higher education, your GPA can plummet in no time, but it takes a lifetime to get it back up.

Unless you are a student who received annual scholarships or renewable grants, you are pretty much on your own in funding your education. After my first year of college, I definitely learned this the hard way. I spent ten semesters at Hampton, unsure how I would pay for this education for eight of them. There were times that I shared books with friends, or they would give me their old books once they completed a course. I would have to make copies of my professors' books or just not have access and pray that I passed with the information that I could gather. Additionally, I would have to bargain with the financial aid office to be cleared for classes and maintain my schedule.

Personally, I also experienced some significant losses during my college tenure. As a sophomore and during the early part of my junior year, I lost three uncles. By the spring of my junior year, my grandmother was diagnosed with pancreatic cancer, and my father passed on March 29, 2011. I was totally destroyed! I did not want to do anything, and my motivation was very low. I would attend classes sparingly but managed to pass six out of my seven classes that semester. As fate would have it, my grandmother passed later that year during the summer. Shortly after that, with my "dad away from home," my choir director would also depart the physical world just a few months later in the fall of my senior year. I was glad to see 2011 leave, to say the least.

Experiencing these deaths so close together really took a toll on me mentally, emotionally, and academically. My grades were tragic and not nearly my best work. In hindsight, this may have been when I first developed my depression; I just did not know it. The following two years were a struggle, but by God's grace, I walked in Hampton's commencement ceremony on May 12, 2013; however, I did not get my degree that day. I still had one more class to complete. Just when I thought the string of tragedies that had plagued my college years was over, I lost a cherished professor; he died two days after my birthday. Despite being brokenhearted, I had made it this far, so not finishing was not an option. I officially became a graduate of Hampton University with a bachelor's degree in English with a concentration in middle and secondary education in August 2013, almost five years to the day of beginning that journey. I eventually enrolled in graduate studies, and, in sixteen short months, I earned a master of arts degree in teaching in English education from Georgia State University on May 7, 2016. Later that year, I began my career as a high school English language arts teacher. 🎓

What is the greatest lesson learned?
Despite everything I endured, I never gave up on myself. If you want something badly enough, go for it. Success has to be a choice despite your circumstances.

What advice would you share with first year college student?
Enjoy yourselves but prioritize your studies and set a solid foundation. There may come a time when things are difficult, either personally or academically, and you need that cushion for your grade point average. Additionally, never stop looking and applying for scholarships and grants throughout your college tenure. Lastly, start networking as soon as you can to build connections for the future.

Nikkia Grant
Hampton University | Class of 2013

THE FINANCING OF LIGHTS, CAMERA, ACTION!

I am New York through and through, so the thought of going away to college never really entered my mind. I was part of a large family, and finances were tight. My older siblings contributed to the household. Incurring college debt was not something that incited me. I graduated from John Dewey high school in Coney Island, Brooklyn, NY. It was a majority Caucasian school, 70-30 split, but we blended well. In high school, I was unsure of what I wanted to study. But after some real-life experience, my area of interest was clear—journalism and broadcasting. I enrolled in Borough of Manhattan Community College (CUNY-BMCC) right out of high school in 1988 to earn an associate of arts in Communications.

As I stepped into young adulthood and my manhood, I earned a new title- Dad! I welcomed a beautiful baby girl in 1990. With this new responsibility, my education had to take a back seat. My focus shifted, and I worked two jobs, one full-time and one part-time, to provide for my daughter and contribute to the household expenses with my mother. Dreams and learning deferred. I re-enrolled in BMCC in 1999 and graduated in 2000. My mother had preached education and the doors which it would open for years. She had returned to school late in life to set the example for my siblings and me, so I knew I wanted more. Wasting no time, I continued my education and enrolled in CUNY-City College of New York. In all honesty, this was my second choice. I wanted to attend New York University (NYU). They have one of the best film programs in the country, but my family's financial commitment did not allow me to pursue it.

I enjoyed myself while I attended City College. I had some amazing professors, like Dr. Leonard Jefferies, renowned intellectual of Black Studies, and I was often challenged in my film classes. I was disappointed because I believed if I had attended NYU, my exposure to film art would have been more comprehensive. NYU, after all, was where Spike Lee and many others had attended.

Unfortunately, I could not take advantage of many extra-curricular activities due to work and family obligations, so my college experience was limited and extended. I had to repeat a few courses that did not transfer from CUNY two-year to CUNY four-year. This was a hard lesson to learn because although I had passed a two-year level course, I needed to have the required final grade not to lose the credits or to be able to apply it to my major. This prolonged graduation and hurt my financial aid. I ran out of financial assistance during my last year of college. At this point, I had a new full-time job where overtime was plentiful, which allowed me to pay for the last two semesters. Now, I had the financial part under control with a new job, but I was limited in taking courses because of my work schedule. It was through true grit and determination that I crossed the graduation finish line. I graduated with a bachelor of arts degree in Communication with a 3.9 GPA. My college experiences provided me with the skillset to produce two short films, *The N-Word, The Racial Apathy or Term of Endearment, and A look Into time.*

What is the greatest lesson learned?
I learned true discipline and determination will help you see things through to completion.

What advice would you share with first year college student?
Apply, apply, and apply for scholarships. Remain focused. Let your learning take you beyond the walls of the classroom. Do not limit yourself.

O. Burton
CUNY-City College | Class of 2004
CUNY-Borough of Manhattan Community College | Class of 2000

TAKE THE LIMITS OFF

High college expectations are standard in South Asian culture. Women are expected to explore the medical field, and men are expected to study engineering. It was no different in my household. I really did not know any other career path outside of the medical field, so secretly, my goal was to major in Pharmacy when I entered college. My academic focus was science, although I struggled all through high school. My parents made me attend William C. Bryant High School; I was not in love with the school. I felt the school lacked the necessary resources to prepare me for college. It was my zone school, and my parents were comfortable knowing I would not have to travel long distances to attend school. At this time, the world was two years post 9-11, I was a Muslim female who wore a hijab, and my parents were concerned for my safety. The limited ability to travel also limited my exposure educationally and socially. I was not the best student by the standards of my culture, but I graduated with an Advanced Regents diploma.

My college plans began to unravel when my father suffered a heart attack and was placed on disability. This put a strain on our family finances and limited my college options. Instead of exploring out-of-state colleges or a Pharmacy College like St. John's University, my search was narrowed to the City University of New York (CUNY). This was the most economically sound decision at that time. I was awarded a scholarship and received additional aid that not only helped me but my family also. I enrolled in Hunter College in 2007, expecting a college experience, but what I experienced felt more like a continuation of high school. I commuted to school, and most of my classes were held in one building; however, there was a stark contrast in the size of the classrooms. My science classes had 500-700 students in one auditorium. I did not know the professors, but they knew me only through the last four digits of my social security number. Needless to say, it required a significant adjustment and was beyond frustrating at times. I remained isolated, I did not utilize the extra resources like office hours, and I was afraid to ask questions for fear of looking stupid. I was suffering because I missed the one-on-one student-teacher relationship from high school. Eventually, I made a few connections and participated in study-hall sessions. Those sessions were helpful, but they were not enough to make a difference.

Honestly, my goal was to make my parents happy and graduate from college. My older brother had attempted college but never completed it, so it was all riding on me, and I really wanted this experience to be over. I felt I was going along to get along, and it took five long years to do so. My area of study was Biochemistry.

This major was not my first choice, but I was so deep into the science curriculum that my choice was to either finish this course of study or start over. I thought to myself, "Start over and do what?" I did not have a clue as to what I really wanted to do. I had entertained the idea of teaching; however, at the time, I could not see how I would transition or merge the two fields. I subsequently figured it out and began to tutor children in the Sciences.

I realize now that I did not take my educational opportunity seriously. Self-esteem issues plagued me throughout high school and my early years of college. I did not explore all that college had to offer; thus, I missed many opportunities. Midway through my college experience, I became more accepting of myself, my hijab and realized people accepted me for who I was. I finally explored and participated in the social aspect of college, which awakened the college experience for me. I am grateful for the connections I made through the Muslim Student Association and the South Asia Association. Many of my fellow students in those organizations are still my friends today.

The day I had been waiting for finally arrived–graduation. Simultaneously I experienced a sense of relief and excitement. I was the first to graduate in my family, and this moment was monumental. Though still unsure of the next steps, I beamed with pride until my face hurt. Yes, I had struggled, but I had finally earned a bachelor of arts degree in biochemistry.

What is the greatest lesson learned?
I am responsible for creating my own future. I have to do what is necessary to succeed. The only person I have to prove anything to is myself.

What advice would you share with first year college student?
Have backup options. Do not be so focused on just one route. Never let life hold you back from what you really want. Get to know professors in class and out of the classroom. Do not let people dictate your career goals. Take care of your mental health.

Anonymous
CUNY- Hunter College | Class of 2012

DR. VEE'S SEEDS FOR THE FINANCIAL MAZE

Following the money in many situations often highlights the problem or the solution. The Financial Maze many students must navigate while in college can create countless detours. However, these stories detail that a detour does not mean derailment. I have witnessed entrepreneurs' birth during their college experience as students learn to be creative in their financial endeavors, from managing semester refund checks, full or part-time employment, on- campus work-study, SGA stipends, etc. Any of these can alleviate the financial strain students may encounter, especially in their last semesters closer to graduation. Research shows financial funding becomes increasingly difficult to obtain during the final semesters after earning 90+ credits.

Here are a few tips:

- Pay yourself first from all refund checks, jobs (full, part-time, or work-study), and scholarships.
- Don't live off credit cards.
- Borrow what you need, not what you want.

SECTION 3
EMOTIONAL WELL-BEING

Feel good…look good! The college experience can be exciting as students live in a new environment, study various courses, and strive to win gold in achieving academic success— graduation. Yet, throughout the years, I have witnessed those very issues become the cause of tremendous stress.

The theme of this section is Emotional Well-being. Finding the balance between life challenges, and managing all of what college life has to offer is the core of emotional well-being. The academic pressures of papers, exams, and the desire to belong may heighten physiological distress or emotional imbalance. These stories underscore the innate desire to overcome the internal and external pressures derived from academics and life. The experiences they thought would have or should have broken them actually built them and made them better. When other self-remedies failed, these students dared to ask and sought help, taking a break, if necessary. They understood that they needed to heal the hole they were experiencing in order to be whole.

To be successful as a student, particularly a college student, an all-inclusive holistic health approach must be a part of the recipe for success.

HEY GOD, WHERE ARE YOU?

My picturesque family seemed just a little shy of perfect. Many of my high school friends called me "lucky" as I was raised in a two-parent household. I would say that "I'm blessed," but it's funny I did not really think it was a big deal until it was. I guess I took my "normal" life for granted, but oh boy, would that change during my college years.

The expectation for me was high— I was the only girl, the oldest child, and neither of my parents or grandparents had graduated from college. I, Aliyah, was the one to make that dream come true for everyone. My pride said I was the shining star, and I was the one to carry the family name across the graduation platform to the finish line.

My initial #1 college was Howard University. I was focused and on track until I wasn't. The possible rejection was not an option for me, so I did not even try. I went with a safe choice and enrolled in SUNY Utica in Fall 2016. My focus not only shifted from the desired school I wanted to attend but also the potential career. For years I knew I wanted to be a teacher. However, I allowed the opinions of others to redirect my interest to the study of law. I declared my major as criminal justice, and I was miserable. Did I say miserable? Utica was not the school I wanted to attend. And, I wasn't studying the area in which I was really passionate. This was compounded with racial microaggressions from students and faculty. I felt lost and out of place. I returned home on the weekend to find a sense of normalcy with friends and my church family. The weekends were too short and the drive back too long; I dreaded it. I think this was the first time that I began to experience depression.

The indirect racial innuendos often made me question myself, fueling my insecurities as one of a handful of African American students on campus. I found myself isolated, dreaming in my room and avoiding the student center. I felt lost; who could I turn to? My loving parents had sacrificed and expected so much, but all I could think was I wanted OUT! I temporarily laid that trusted companion of pride aside and confided in my pastor, the late Rev. Dr. J.G. McCann. I often went to him, so this was nothing new. A very well-educated man himself, quitting was not an option. He would often say, "If you don't quit, you'll make it." I knew I would hear that during our conversation. He was a safe place for me. So, his guidance was a jewel. He helped me break the news of leaving Utica College to my parents. I could sense the disappointment, but I had a plan B. I applied to all of CUNY's four-year schools. My #1 choice was Hunter College, but my sure thing was Lehman. To my surprise, Hunter was the only school that even responded—Look at God! So, I was ready to do this again. I transferred to Hunter College in September 2017, and this time, I declared my truth, education as my major.

All seemed to be going well, but I realized it was much more difficult staying focused on schoolwork now that I was a commuter student. I had what I wanted, family, church family, a boyfriend, and a slight social life. I quickly realized the importance of managing my time. I pressed forward with my studies, adjusting to this new normal.

One day as I sat in Spanish 202, I was interrupted by a phone call from my mother followed by a text which was not unusual. But, the purpose of this call and text was different. There was an urgency to the message. "Taking dad to the hospital." I immediately walked out of class and headed straight to the hospital only to learn that what we thought was a mild fever had turned critical.

The doctors informed us to begin to make final arrangements. WHAT?! WAIT! What was really happening right now? Moments ago, I was a normal college student. Now I was being told to think about burying my father. God, this could not be! We called our pastor, who prayed. My father's situation improved from life-threatening to having his lower right leg being amputated. The goal was to save my father's life, so he had to lose his leg from the knee down. His pride caused him to adamantly refuse at first. I pleaded with my father; I was not ready to lose him.

The road was not easy, but I knew I had to be there for my dad. My two-parent household was already strained by other mounting issues, and this did not help. In a matter of months, I was a college student, a big sister, and now a caregiver and substitute mother as the reality of the two-parent household had come to a screeching halt. I took an unofficial two-month leave from school. My professors at Hunter were the best. My pastor and doctors attested to the traumatic incident I had endured, so my professors could give me an "Incomplete" instead of failing grades. I was a junior in college, and this was the first time I had heard that an incomplete was even an option.

Through it all, I was able to mask my depression with busyness, but it soon became too much for me. I barely attended church, and when I did, I was verbally abusive to people. In some instances, I was willing to get physical. This was further compounded with another traumatic event in summer 2019. My world, my confidant, my pastor took his last breath on what was supposed to be a fun-filled cruise. It seemed like time stopped on the cruise when I saw his lifeless body was a horrible experience. How could God be so cruel? I sank into a hole of darkness, it consumed me, and I lashed out in anger. I was even angry with God. My spiritual father, mentor, confidant GONE! In addition, my dad was not the same man because a piece of him was missing physically. As I looked into his eyes, I would see the emotional pain of the end of a 20+ year marriage, and I would think he too was mad with God. My pride would not let me totally fall apart; everyone needed me. "Who cares what you think?" was a recurring thought, and it was apparent in my behavior.

I was angry all the time. God took my pastor, and my parents dismantled and disrupted the family with their decision to get divorced. Crossing the graduation finish line was not at the top of my list. Even though I could see God in the midst of all these struggles, God redirected my steps (Psalms 32:8) through Overseer McCann, Pastor McCann's widow. Her encouragement motivated me to lend my skill set to the church during the pandemic. I found strength, purpose, and JOY Pastor McCann would also say, "Jesus, Others, and Yourself will give you JOY." This joy gave me the strength to finish my last year of college. I switched majors from Education to English and graduated with a 3.30 GPA in the middle of the COVID-19 pandemic. My teaching dream is now a reality. Throughout my college journey, I have grown emotionally and spiritually. Through counseling, I found my voice, and I know how to express it in a positive light.

What is the greatest lesson learned?
Always follow your heart. Never allow present circumstances to stop me from going after what I know and want. If there's a school I want to attend, a program I want to be a part of, whatever the case may be, I apply regardless of what I have, and trust that if it's for me, it will happen.

What advice would you share with first year college student?
Never be afraid to ask questions. The only dumb questions are the ones that go unasked; it's important to seek help whether it's with schoolwork, declaring a major, even if it's a question on how to find your next class— don't be afraid to ask for help! Asking questions will save you a lot of lost time, and you'll then be able to use the knowledge you gained to help the next person. Utilize every resource that is provided to you and rely on your team/village for support.

Aliyah-Simone
Hunter College-CUNY | Class of 2020

EDUCATION BEYOND OUR BORDERS; DREAMS DO COME TRUE

The plan was to attend a college where I felt challenged and at home, and Howard University was my choice. When I visited Howard University, I was able to see a reflection of myself throughout the campus, from the arts to the social aspects. My college counselor in high school wasn't aware about the Historically Black College and University (HBCU) culture and said that I should not go. That, plus wanting to know more about myself, drove me to want to attend this HBCU even more. I enrolled at Howard University in 2015. My college experience opened me up to so many things. One of my college takeaways was my freedom.

I had to gain a new sense of responsibility and find a balance as I felt like an adult and a child at the same time. At first, I was very emotional; I was unsure and anxious about being unsuccessful. Little to my knowledge, I did come to love the workload I received from my professors. I found new ways to be vulnerable in my creative processes. I opened myself up to taking on acting roles and creative writing pieces I usually wouldn't think I would be involved in.

Another thing I enjoyed most was the family I made. I took a bold move and walked up to two girls and made them my friends for life. There was an instant connection; the vibe was authentic. I had never done anything like that before—I just walked up and introduced myself. These new friendships made exploring the city a new adventure. We would party till 4 a.m., have movie marathons, play cards, and video games. It was like being back at home with my brother, just enjoying time as a kid. This experience helped with my adjustment to college.

College comes with challenges academically, socially, and even mentally, and it was no different for me. I focused and determined to finish and hand in all my tasks and projects on time without losing my mind. In spring 2017, there was a traumatic incident where I thought I was going to die. There's no need for specifics, but I went home to be with my family after the incident. It was the family connection that gave me the strength to return to school. I didn't want to be the victim and fall behind on my work. I avoided the feelings that I had and pretended it never happened. Unfortunately, that semester ended with a bunch of C's and a few A's. My previous average was a 4.0, I was disappointed with myself. My closest friend told me that she was proud of me for pushing through the semester; however, she insisted that I take some time and focus on myself. I had to be reflective and do a reality check, I was not defined by my grades, nor would I let it rule over my sanity.

Some of the struggles with my college academics were a result of my high school experience. College differed considerably in comparison to high school. I did the bare minimum in high school and achieved high grades, but now was time to put in work. It was hard finding a strategy that best worked for me. At the beginning of my junior year, I found new strategies that helped me acclimate and achieve my academic goals. The only thing I found that worked for me was isolating myself from all distractions. I would find hidden locations in the library where no one else would be and would work so freely. I was able to achieve the best outcomes on every project I worked on from there on out. It was just me, my laptop, and the peaceful meditation music in my ears. Creating a color-block calendar in Google Sheets was extremely beneficial to keep me on track with study/homework and extracurricular activities.

Even though things got a little rough while I was at college, I drew comfort from my family. I came from a loving family who were constantly thinking about me, even if I didn't call them once a week. Keeping up with assignments, managing time, and activities, I sometimes felt like I was swamped. Time escaped me, and I would forget to call home. My mom called me, my father called, and to my surprise, even my brother called a few times. When I felt alone the most, they were always there to remind me that they loved me and were there as support. I loved them deeply and appreciated all the efforts they made to make me feel special, grounded, and focused on the finish line. Even though the finish line was in sight, I still had more of my college experience to unpack. And I did so in the summer of 2018, my education became global, not just from reading facts and figures out of a textbook, but actual experience.

I was able to attend a Study Abroad program in Prague, Czech Republic. I thought traveling to Washington DC. was a challenge, but going overseas to Europe was the most significant milestone in my college career. I lived in an apartment with seven other college students from different institutions. I got to explore many things and aspects in the beautiful city of Prague with my friends. I also traveled to Berlin, Germany, Vienna, Austria, and Amsterdam in the Netherlands. I was very fortunate to have this experience and learned of the culture of all these places. Through a scholarship, I had the opportunity to make YouTube videos of my adventures in Europe, where I felt like Dora the Explorer, bringing my childhood dreams of traveling to life. My takeaway from this experience was that I developed a skill and passion for videography, broadening my horizons and others who would see my work.

The day of graduation was a complete blur. While I don't remember many of my professors talking at the podium, I remember the sweltering heat that existed in the gymnasium. It was a hot day in May of 2019, and it felt like I had escaped a sauna. When my family embraced me after I had received my diploma, I experienced a true moment of relief from what I had felt over the past four years. I didn't have to worry about the next group project, the next deadline, or the next performance I had to do. I felt like I had finally achieved one of my lifelong goals. I could literally feel my environment shifting.

What is the greatest lesson learned?
College was a gauge of my determination. And I learned the importance of maintaining my mental health while balancing academic performance as well. It is almost impossible to achieve anything without having a stable mindset and support system. The journey was a success because of the village, that surrounded me.

What advice would you share with first year college student?
Believe that everyone has their own separate path. College is a reality check in understanding that there are many ways to complete your tasks and goals. This is a time not to limit yourself, regardless of your own doubts. Over time you will flourish and break through a mold you would have never expected. I achieved one of my childhood goals of going backpacking around Europe and receiving my college degree at the same time. This experience was a worthwhile one, and I'm thankful to everyone for their support and confidence in me.

Nia Alysse Seaton
Howard University | Class of 2019

I AM MORE THAN MY SKIN COLOR

My mother had always provided me with opportunities, and receiving an education was no different. The options created a great foundation, but often my difference, my blackness, was highlighted. Believing college would open doors for me to start adulthood, I attended the College of Staten Island. Also, I wanted to broaden my knowledge and education. I picked my school because it gave me balance; it was close enough while still creating distance from home. I was familiar with the area from my childhood visits.

So here I was, an eager high school graduate ready to take on the world. However, the journey started off a little rocky. During college, I encountered and overcame more racist challenges than I thought I would in 2016. The challenges were different in college than they were in middle school and high school. In college, it was not subtle racism. It was more apparent and in your face. I was so uncomfortable I went home every weekend; thus, I was not really enjoying my college experience. I made the decision to transfer to East Stroudsburg University. I thought the distance would not only grant me a new environment but perspective. To my surprise, I encountered classmates who had never had close encounters with someone who was African American or of African decedent. The biggest shock was in my first two months after arriving on campus. There were people with confederate flags in their room or car stickers. WHAT! I never fathomed that people who believed in the confederacy attended the same school and shared the same space. My mother's sorority sisters (Delta Sigma Theta Sorority, Inc.) were an outlet. They made sure I was okay and gave me a sense of comfort.

My new school was "supposed" to be the most diverse out of all State schools in Pennsylvania. One of the most dreadful experiences I had on campus was during my sophomore year. I heard my neighbors say, "Black people shouldn't be allowed to go to school," "Trump can grab my p***y," and "certain Black people were only accepted into schools because of affirmative action." I remember my roommate and I went to their door because that was the last straw for us. Our neighbors ignored us and did not respond to repeated knocking on the door. Our goal was to have a conversation about their comments, "Black people shouldn't be allowed in Universities." Instead, they attempted to shift the blame and lied to the Resident Assistant (RA) that we were "harassing them." The RA knew their statement was not factual because we had complained about them before. I also brought this matter up when I was interviewed to be Resident Assistant that same year. The RA also told them, "You have to realize that these walls are thin, and people can hear what you say." That was the last day I heard any racist comments from them, but there were intimidation attempts when my roommate and I would see them around campus. They would point us out to others. It no longer bothered me, they had been exposed, and I had the receipts. Our neighbors were emboldened by who was in the White House at the time. It is my hope they learned their lesson.

Through all the drama, I made great friends and had wonderful experiences during my college years. One such time was meeting new people from different places in the world. I was able to travel/study abroad in Europe during my sophomore year. This experience transformed my life. I enjoyed my social life, and my freedom was at an all-time high. I think every person who has the opportunity to travel, even if it's only an hour away, should do it. Campus life has its ups and downs, but it is what you make of it. I was abroad for two months. I traveled immediately after finals concluded in Spring 2017. It was a fantastic experience that I would not trade for anything because I could create friendships with people from different parts of the world. I now have friends from Canada, France, Switzerland, and Germany! I have visited almost all of them, or they have visited New York to see me.

The goal of college is to obtain a degree. However, a huge personal achievement during my college experience was finding a job that paid for my room and board, an internship, and traveling. I became a Resident Assistant my last two years attending college, which had its ups and downs as any job would. My social life was almost nonexistent, and working on the weekends was the most challenging because anything and everything could happen and did happen. A weekend of peace was a rarity, fire alarms going off because someone "burned popcorn or ramen," which I later found out was how students got rid of the marijuana smell. The best were the phone calls from people locked out at 3 a.m. or 4 a.m. These were some of the worst nights because the ringer would give me a headache. Other issues included arguments between residents, the noise level, and unwanted guests. The list can go on. There was never a typical weekend as a Resident Assistant. These incidents and others taught me excellent communication, mediation, and time management skills, to name a few. These have been skills I have taken into my life after college.

I looked forward to graduation. The eager high school student had now become the eager college graduate who wanted out of this experience and was ready to create a new normal that wasn't so hostile. I am grateful for a supportive mother and family. They have been my support system throughout times of self-doubt, experiencing bouts of stress-related illnesses throughout my tenure at college, mental and physical exhaustion, and tears. I did my best to shield my mother from knowing how much I went through. The old saying "a mother knows" is absolutely correct! My mother and stepfather would drive to my college campus to hand-deliver care packages and take me out to dinner in a heartbeat, which was very therapeutic for me. This support was the fuel I needed to graduate with a bachelor of arts degree in marketing with a minor in communication and a 3.2 GPA. 🎓

What is the greatest lesson learned?
Don't let other people's obstacles dictate your destiny. Always keep a good head on your shoulders because I know the difference between right and wrong.

What advice would you share with first year college student?
Be your own leader—lead by your own example, join clubs, and go to socials (if you live in the dorms). That's how you make friends and have a balance between your social and educational life.

S.O.
East Stroudsburg University | Class of 2019

MIND OVER MATTER

I often second guess myself, overlooking accomplishments in favor of spending hours contemplating times in my life when I might have done things differently. When I could have done better or somehow tried harder. If I try hard enough, maybe I can pinpoint when I began to fail at living up to expectations? I notice when this happens, I have to force my brain to stop. Ruminating like this is always counterproductive for me. Instead, I remind myself to acknowledge the obstacles I overcame, obstacles that helped make me stronger.

I started my freshman year of college at the University of Delaware the first fall after graduating from high school. It took me ten years before I finally completed my bachelor's degree. In those ten years, I tried out four different higher education institutions and a wide variety of majors (including fashion merchandising!). I felt an underlying uncertainty of not having a clear (or even blurry!) vision of the career I would find most fulfilling. Less than two years later, I found myself in the hospital emergency room for the first of what would be three psychiatric hospitalizations in a year. Barely an adult, I now had a psychiatric diagnosis and zero desire to accept it. My mind went on haunting me, mocking my efforts, causing me to doubt my ability to do anything at all. Because of my inability to deal with severe symptoms, I behaved in ways that I am now embarrassed to even think about. All the while, I pushed the people closest to me away. It was never intentional, but I was struggling inside and out, to the point that I was impossible to be around.

Looking back, signs that something was wrong started showing up around the time I finished high school. At that time, I had a great group of friends I had not yet pushed out of my life and still lived at home: I managed to avert any major crises. I graduated at the top of my class, oblivious to the impending breakdown waiting for me just around the corner. After my initial hospitalization, I struggled to accept the reality that my life had drastically changed. It took me several years to fully accept that this was not going to go away. And, despite the challenges I'd face moving forward, I was still the same person inside. While I was coming to terms with this, I moved back home. Only then did I begin to realize the extent to which my parents were my strongest advocates. On my worst days, they never gave up on me, and I am sure that I was not pleasant to be around. I continued struggling with symptoms, and the medications that were designed to help me often came with intolerable side effects. Together, my parents supported me unconditionally, and because of them, I began to believe in myself again.

I re-enrolled in school, this time trying out the criminal justice program at Delaware Technical Community College. I took smaller classes where there was more interaction between the students and the instructors. We discussed issues that affected society as a whole, and my passion for learning reemerged. Then slowly, my confidence that I'd be able to graduate reemerged.

At home, my parents committed to their own learning as I worked through Del Tech's program. I graduated with the highest honors in December 2011 and continued on to get my bachelor's degree after that. Meanwhile, they dove into anything and everything that could help them understand my illness and how to help me manage it. Life doesn't always give you what you want. It gives you what you need to survive. The path I'd envisioned–finishing school in four years, getting a steady job, finding a relationship–didn't happen. I went off the beaten path, and at first, found it challenging to navigate. Now that I've found my way, I appreciate the beauty around me. I learned to find my own way and go at my own pace, thanks to my incredible support system. I look back and realize what I learned on my journey to a degree were valuable lessons, both inside and out of the classroom. Some of my favorite life lessons from that time are listed here.

What are the greatest lessons learned?
Make health a non-negotiable priority. This includes both mind and my body. People who want the best for you are a treasure. Find the opportunity to learn from frustrations or setbacks, grieve when you need to, and then try again.

What advice would you share with first year college student?
Doing your best doesn't mean you need to be the best. Don't put undue pressure on yourself, and give yourself credit when credit is due. When you want to give up, don't!

Megan Sokola
Wilmington University | Class of 2013
Delaware Technical College | Class of 2011

HE HEARD MY CRY!

I never wanted to go to college. In fact, my life's goal was to get pregnant at 18. This is the mentality I had growing up in the hood. I saw the four walls of the projects, and I thought, "This is all there is to life." Then in my junior year of high school, all of my friends turned on me. I was devastated; they started bullying me, cyberbullying me, and calling me hurtful names. I needed to escape. So, college became my escape, and it is where I got a fresh start.

I strongly desired to attend college out of state to escape the torment of home. My top two choices were Howard University and Clark Atlanta. However, my Guidance Counselor advised me that financially SUNY Albany was the better choice. Reluctantly, I obliged, and in the long run, it really did benefit me as I managed to pay off my undergraduate loans six years after graduating. So, I packed my bags and headed to SUNY Albany—Home of the Great Danes—UA! U Know! I'd like to say life got easier, but I was bullied by my roommates in my freshman year. I was constantly in fights. I had no peace, and I just didn't understand why women hated me. I remember praying to God to get me out of these toxic friendships.

After my freshman year, God answered. I was able to live apart from my former friends. With the drama behind me, I made new friends. We called ourselves The Sister Circle. We were 11 Black women with similar backgrounds looking to enjoy our college experience.

I was very active on campus. I went to events, led campus groups, started a mentorship group for high school students, intending to expose them to college early on. I volunteered at an HIV clinic, and I studied abroad. I attended American Intercontinental University in London, UK. While there, I studied English and London History. I got to explore a new city, meet my British family for the first time, and travel to Spain and Rome. It was an unforgettable experience. Even with such an opportunity, the depression followed me. I was so depressed. I was an academic scholar on the Dean's List, inducted into the National Society for Collegiate Scholars (NSCS), Chi Alpha Epsilon, National Honor Society, and Omicron Delta Kappa Society. Still, awards and honors could not take away the pain. The internal ache was ever-present, even on the brightest day.

About my junior year, I woke up one morning to a disturbing call from my grandmother. My favorite aunt's body was found in Jamaica. It seemed like a suicide. My initial thought was, "I'm next," as if suicide was running deep within my family, looking for its next victim. My depression got worse, and my closest girlfriends didn't want to be around me. I felt abandoned and confused.

I remember one night in my senior year; I was so tired of masking the pain. I wanted to finally be free. I grabbed a handful of pills, and I knelt on the floor, crying out to God. In all honesty, I did not want to end my life, but what was the alternative? The deep gaping hole of darkness left me feeling so empty on the inside. Who would notice me? Who would miss me? I struggled as I slowly brought the pills to my mouth, and then there was a loud knock at my apartment door. I quickly put the pills away and wiped my tears. My best girlfriend surprised me. To this day, she doesn't know that she saved my life. From that day on, I poured my energy into my senior year activities. I never sought counseling because it never crossed my mind to do it. Was the darkness gone? No, but for that moment, I decided to live and not die, and not share my truth.

Aside from depression, I thrived in college. I was part of the Educational Opportunity Program (EOP). I would receive additional resources to purchase books in my freshman and sophomore years. I also had college advisors who helped me with everything from selecting classes to crafting the perfect resume. Work-study to offset campus living expenses was also a benefit of EOP I was an RA for one year, so my room was free, and there I learned valuable counseling skills that I still use in my career today.

My greatest achievement in college was starting a mentor group for high school students. It was called Dream Organization. We went into the local high schools, helped them with homework, brought them on campus, and helped prepare them for college. I'm not sure if the group still exists, but it was going strong after I graduated in 2009.

Graduation brought on its own set of issues; I felt a mix of emotions as the realization that the little world I had lived in for 4 years was over. I had become accustomed to my friends living close, going to class in pajamas, working out in the middle of the day, and partying all weekend. Then in the blink of an eye, I was a graduate and thrust into the real world with no real direction. I learned a lot in college. I gained my independence, learned how to interact with people of diverse backgrounds, and learned how to negotiate my grades, which later spilled into negotiating my salary. It is true; college skills become life skills.

My college years opened my eyes to the fact that there is a whole world out there, and I don't have to feel trapped in the housing projects. Living in the housing projects didn't define me. It drives me to change the trajectory of my life. I have a purpose! I matter! And so do you, who will read this. I am grateful I eventually overcame depression in my late 20s because God reminded me of my purpose. I'm actually pleased that I didn't end my life in my senior year. Because if I did, I wouldn't be here sharing my story with you.

What is the greatest lesson learned?
College is a time of discovery. All of life's answers may not be revealed, but college is a piece of the puzzle.

What advice would you share with first year college student?
My advice to college students is to enjoy it! Embrace the culture, study abroad, go to parties, enjoy the all-night study sessions, take on internships, and become leaders in college groups. Every decision you make in college affects your adult life. In addition to academics, you learn life skills. You gain memories that will help shape your early adult life and foster valuable relationships that may last a lifetime. If you struggle with depression, ASK FOR HELP! You don't have to go through it on your own.

Shamara "Star" Cox
SUNY Albany | Class of 2009

I AM ENOUGH!

I am a first-generation American and was one of the first in my family to attend college in America. In a West Indian family, not going to college was not an option. It was a given that you would go to college; just where you would go and what you would study was a mystery. I knew what I wanted to study since my 10th Grade in High School at Brooklyn Tech. After attending an Engineering Conference held by the National Society of Black Engineers, I found my purpose. I was so excited to know what I wanted to do; I told my math teacher that I wanted to be an Engineer. My excitement was tainted with his response, "Some people shouldn't have such lofty goals."

In utter disbelief, I responded, "What do you mean by that?"

His reply, "If you build a bridge, make sure you put your name on it in bold letters, so I know not to cross it," was my introduction to microaggression behavior. The nerve!

He did not even realize his limited thinking. I had no desire to be a civil engineer and no interest in building anything. Engineers did so much more! Motivated by his dismissiveness, I informed him that I will become an Engineer and attend the school that built Engineers, Rensselaer Polytechnic Institute. His retort, "Your chances of getting into RPI are nil, but good luck." This encounter told me that haters are real. If I didn't have the love of my family who cared for me and other teachers who encouraged me, I might have believed him. I also knew I couldn't share this incident with my mother, as the repercussions would not have been good for anyone. Even years after the fact, it doesn't sit well with her or other family members.

Rensselaer Polytechnic Institute was an experience like no other. Founded in 1824, the oldest Technological University in the English-speaking world. It is a school with a 3 to 1 Male to Female ratio and 6% POC and 94% Caucasian. Where would I fit in? I would walk into classrooms and be 1 of 2 Black people and often the only woman. I was constantly dismissed and overlooked. I'd sit in classes with young men who would say to my face, "Women don't belong as Engineers." They also would say that the only reason I was there was because of affirmative action. White Supremacy and disdain for people of color were rampant and a natural thing like breathing. I was encouraged to see someone who looked like me at the helm of the institution.

However, the RPI President, Shirley Ann Jackson, a Black Woman, however, was often disrespected and disregarded. We'd read Opens in the school newspaper that allowing more students of color into RPI was like letting the squirrels in for the sake of diversity. This was 2004, not 1955, yet we still had blatant racism, sexism, and an environment that felt fraught with tension.

I came from a high-performing high school with a stellar reputation, and going to RPI is where I first encountered what it felt like to fail. At RPI, it was there that I understood what it felt like to be an outsider. RPI is known as the "Meat Grinder." If one could make it out of there, you are a prime cut of meat; if you don't, you're the byproduct. Having attended Brooklyn Tech, I thought I was prepared for what I'd face at RPI I was wrong. I would walk into the classrooms and would feel like I fell down a rabbit hole. I thought I knew what it meant to study, but I really didn't. I made it through school my entire life by going to class and paying attention, but at RPI, it wasn't like that. They fully depended on the book to teach us what we needed to know without covering what would be tested in class at all. I was like a castaway adrift at sea. Microaggressive commentary from classmates compounded this. They would look at me like I was a different species and ask questions like, "Have you ever been around this many white people before?" or "You're from NYC. Were you in a gang?" In my first two years, I struggled.

I mustered through with mediocre grades, but I was determined I wouldn't quit. I clearly remember sitting in my Advisors office in the Minority Student Affairs Office, lamenting to her that I wasn't smart enough to be there. Her eyes got wide, and you could hear a pin drop. Then she said through gritted teeth, close the door. I closed the door, and I swear her head spun like the exorcist. She looked at me and said, "Don't you ever let me hear you say that you are not smart enough to be here. You are here for a reason, and you will finish what you started." Words of Black administrators would keep me bolstered as I continued my journey at RPI.

In my Junior year, I had a lapse in judgment. I was sick of trying to keep my head above water, and at the urging of one of the program directors, I changed my major. She told me that I should just do something easier if I wanted to graduate. She stated that if I didn't switch to something else, I could possibly lose out on some of the funding I received to attend. Others, such as my mother, advisor, told me not to do it. I didn't listen. For one semester, I switched my major, the consequence put me behind in my Engineering curriculum. The classes offered only in the Spring were missed out on because I switched my major. Changing my major for that semester delayed me almost a year.

I barely went to class, only showed up for tests, and that semester I had a 3.75 GPA. The classes weren't easy, but I could do this work in my sleep compared to the classes I was taking prior. Even though it was an easier academic path, I was bored, so I switched my major back to my original goal, Engineering. The decision to switch back to Engineering was pivotal. It charted a course to one of the most phenomenal career experiences at NBC Sports. I had the opportunity to work on the Olympics, travel the world, and become an Emmy award winner using the skills I learned at RPI I would have missed these and so many other opportunities if I had quit engineering. I often think, "If I had quit, where would I be now?"

I felt a strong sense of pride when I walked across the stage in 2009. It is easily one of the happiest moments of my life. I came out of it having earned my "E." This was a phrase used by Engineering graduates because the title "Engineer" is earned, not given as in some job titles like Sanitation Engineer. This is the gold star! Earned, not given!

I knew it was God's grace that sustained and kept me. I walked out of RPI with a dual degree in Industrial Engineering and Psychology. God provided me with the strength and conviction that I AM Enough, I AM Smart enough, and He equipped me to succeed. I returned in 2010 to RPI to complete my master of science degree in business management.

What is the greatest lesson learned?
To let my inner strength be my guiding force. Never let the opinion and the opposition that anyone has of you determine your path forward in life.

What advice would you share with first year college student?
Believe in yourself, bet on yourself. Don't Quit! You will want to quit, but if you press on, you will win. Don't be too prideful to ask for help. There are resources to help you to succeed if only you take the time to look for them. You have the tools to succeed. Fearfully and wonderfully made, you have been imbued with the power to overcome any obstacle that is in your way. You are enough!

Denisha S. McPherson
Rensselaer Polytechnic Institute | Class of 2009

DR. VEE'S SEEDS FOR EMOTIONAL WELL-BEING

Colleges and universities that create a culture that embraces mental and emotional wellness promote student success. It has been my experience and research has shown that students who experience depression, anxiety, and other psychological disorders perform more poorly in class. Depressed and anxious students are also more likely to be absent, take semesters off, or drop out of school. When students drop out due to psychological concerns, everyone loses, including the student and their future aspirations, the institution and its ratings, its loss of tuition and alumni dollars, and its impact and void on the campus culture, because you, the student, are valued and needed.

The benefits of emotional well-being for students are countless when students engage in things they like to do, have strong relationships, commit to at least 30 minutes of activity daily i.e., dance, intramural sports, going for a walk, and daily positive affirmation.

SECTION 4
SELF-DISCOVERY

The college experiences will introduce students to many dynamics from exploring new places, new courses, and cultures to name a few. When students fully embrace the college experience, they will embark on the theme of this section is self-discovery. One might argue self-discovery happens at various stages of ones' life. However, there are no clear markers to identify when or how. I think, and I believe many would agree, the college years are undoubtedly a time of self-discovery.

The power of relationships whether it be with self or others is a powerful and fulfilling path during the academic journey and life. During this time I have had the privilege to see students flourish as they begin to determine their needs, advocate for themselves, adapt to the ever-changing environment. College becomes a safe space for self-discovery; it is the time and place when students can learn from their mistakes but more importantly lean into the lessons from those mistakes.

These stories emphasize students who took various paths of self-discovery; they discovered that they do not have to repeat history but can create a new family history, the world is bigger than a 10-block radius and they were now a part of a global stage, and boldness and confidence to speak up and speak out. All transpired during the college years and opened students up to endless possibilities which transformed their lives for the better.

FINDING SELF THROUGH EDUCATION

My outlook on college life was that it would never be easy, but deep down, I knew there was a pathway to more. Being mixed but primarily Black and Latino, my cultural background had an unspoken rule, but demonstrated in behavior, that people like us do not go to college. My parents perpetrated this, my mother only had an eighth-grade education, and my father might have finished high school. I had no idea how but I needed to break this generational lack of education. I attended Manchester Regional High School in NJ, right outside of Patterson. Truthfully, I didn't have the best grades, so I knew I'd be relying on my student-athletic abilities and extracurriculars to get into college; I was the football and track team captain and was active in a plethora of clubs. I didn't care which college I attended. The only thing that mattered to me was getting accepted. I applied to Montclair State University and Notre Dame, which I knew was a longshot, but my girlfriend at the time was applying, so I figured, "Hey, why not!" I was rejected by both; however, I finally settled and enrolled in William Paterson University (WPU) in Fall 2011.

WPU. was about a mile away from my high school. Due to its close proximity and the many familiar faces from high school and the neighborhood, it felt like high school part II. My expectations were low. I came from a poor family, so I knew I could not live on campus in the dorm, and driving to campus was not an option, so walking was my form of exercise.

I focused on my studies; high school would not be the defining moment for me. I did well. I was proud of myself. During my two-year term, I earned a respectable 3.56 GPA. However, I was not only attending classes but working two part-time jobs. During the week, I worked 35 hours at a minimum paying job that I absolutely hated. And during the weekends, I worked another 30 hours cleaning and servicing pools, which I enjoyed.

Two part-time jobs and school were beyond exhausting. I primarily supported my girlfriend and could afford a studio apartment for her and her little sister away from their verbally abusive alcoholic mother. Eventually, it all caught up with me in my sophomore year; it became necessary to take a break from my studies. The intention was to take a break for a year, a year that turned into two. I ignored all my student loans, primarily because I did not have the money to repay them, nor the knowledge on how to do so even if I wanted to. My plan was to get back into school as soon as possible. In the meantime, my credit score took a significant hit and dropped into the 300s'. It took years of hard work to regain a respectable score.

I decided to return to college after my first two-year hiatus. I had to figure out who other than me was going to pay for college. I attempted to enroll in the Army; however, I had a skin condition that disqualified me from enlisting. This solidified my already growing feelings of being useless.

Shortly after, I had a horrible breakup with my girlfriend of six years, in which my mother played a role. Since then, I have not seen or spoken with either of them. Though difficult, there was no love loss, at least not in losing my mother. My mother's negative outlook on life and unsupportive nature was because of her trauma throughout her life. All of this led to bouts of depression; it was a tough, lonely time. I felt unproductive and was drinking all day while working overnight shifts. I desperately needed a new environment, so I set my sights on New York City. I found a job I enjoyed, despite the minimal pay, it required no formal skills. I canvased the street for the Human Rights Campaign (HRC) for the LGBTQIA+ community.

Without my degree, I knew I would not advance in this position or any other. It was 2015, and I was now in NYC, living a better life and meeting new friends. One of whom was attending Manhattan College—I visited the campus, applied, and enrolled for the 2015-2016 academic school year. I was excited to receive an almost full-academic scholarship; ninety percent was covered. I would still need to come up with $5,000 to enroll that year. I was beyond frustrated that another opportunity could slip right through my fingers.

I had been estranged from my fathers' side of my family most of my life. Meeting them after my high school graduation was a pleasant surprise, while equally complex. My father convinced my grandfather to pay my outstanding tuition balance allowing me to continue my education endeavors. I was grateful. Everything should have been great, right? The complete opposite, the mental anguish I felt from the abandonment of my girlfriend, and my mother continued to fuel my depression. I quickly found myself unable to get out of bed for days at a time. By the end of that year, I had failed almost every class and my GPA, which was once over a 3.5, was now a pitiful 1.5. I dropped out again. Only, this time I thought it might be for good.

The journey did not have been so difficult. But, I failed to take advantage of counseling services, which probably would have helped me manage my depression and academics. Nor was I directed to these services. Though frustrated, I sought a silver lining. From 2016-2018, I was determined to get my life back on track. The goal was to surround myself with positive people and take time to reflect and refocus. I worked several jobs that merely served as a placeholder yet allowed me to save money and rebuild myself physically, emotionally, and even spiritually. I finally had a chance to heal both my personal and generational traumas.

It was time for a change. In 2018 I re-enrolled in college yet again, this time at Berkeley College in Manhattan. I felt more comfortable at Berkeley, where I was a better fit with the student population. Berkeley had more non-traditional students in their mid-twenties and up who were professionals with the desire to complete the degree which had eluded them until now. Here I found that the professors had a desire to educate and empower students. All was going well!

Berkeley, unlike most institutions, operates on a tri-semester basis, thus allowing me to complete more classes in a shorter amount of time. Then the disruption that turned the world upside down, COVID-19 (March 2020), forced all learning online. I was not new to online learning, but it is not my preferred learning style. I missed the connection garnered from in-person learning. I felt unprepared for this huge transition. One of the major hurdles was the lack of physical technology and stable Wi-Fi, which was once available until the COVID-19 pandemic forced all libraries and secondary support centers to shut down.

My journey drew to a close! I had started and stopped numerous times—transferred, lost credits, changed my major multiple times, including everything from undecided to being an athletic trainer, pre-physical therapy, sports science, IT management, and finally general business. Eventually, the outcome I had always desired, I graduated with a bachelor of arts degree in business administration and a final GPA of 3.7 in Dec 2020. Accomplishing this goal will set me up to take my education further. During this journey, I was lucky to discover who I was and wanted to be. In more ways than one, I defied destiny. 🎓

What is the greatest lesson learned?
Where you start in life does not dictate where one will go or how far one can go.

What advice would you share with first year college student?
Be prepared to manage the system. Don't let the system manage you. Do not be afraid to push and maneuver into spaces where you do not see people who look or sound like you, your mere presence there will create opportunities for others.

Davonte T. Williams
Berkeley College | Class of 2020

THE VILLAGE BEYOND HOME

The question of college was not "if" but "where?" I am grateful for my family. We started the conversation early, somewhere around my sophomore/junior year in high school. Even though I wasn't sure about my college choice just yet, it was clear I wanted and needed to escape the suburban lifestyle of Westchester County. I was seeking a big city experience. Equally as clear was my intended major, Business. We know it's money that makes the world go around, and I wanted to be a part of it but didn't yet know how it would all unfold. I visited colleges with my family in Connecticut, Pennsylvania, DC. I wanted to be away but not too far away. On one of these many college trips, I decided where to pursue my studies and begin to find myself a young man.

In 2013, I decided on Temple University. Temple University has one of the best business schools in the country, The Richard J Fox Business School. However, it was not just the school; it was the people, the whole vibe, which helped me choose Temple after the visit.

I enrolled at Temple University in 2015. It's easy to get lost figuratively and literally; among a 40,000 student population making friends and networking became an essential life savior. As I began to figure out who I was from high school to college. There were various things I had to figure out—what do I do with all this free time? My classes were no longer back-to-back, and sometimes I had an entire day free. Though not too familiar with time management, I realized implementing a scheduling practice would keep me sane but provide balance too: classes, homework, and studying, plus extracurricular activities.

My freshman year was mapped out for me. My advisor was great! Shortly after, it got real; the responsibilities increased from sophomore to junior year. This was the time when I began to establish relationships with the Professors and Advisor, which helped tremendously. I made it a point to visit them during office hours. Even if I only had one question, that question would lead to life-lesson conversations. As a result of one of those conversations, I landed an internship doing digital marketing for local bars and gyms.

Creating a support system via fellow students, professors, some I still speak to this day, served as a village of support through some of the challenging times while in college. This support helped me to think and do things differently. I didn't really know I needed to do things differently; high school practices do not always translate well in college. I had to develop a new thought process. How do

I graduate from this college experience differently-evolved, if I did not come out of my comfort zone? To grow, I had to get involved. I joined the Black Student Union and the American Marketing Association. I took advantage of all available resources, i.e., the career center for resume development and mock interviews. These interviews prepared me for the job I have now and the career I will be stepping into at Subaru America.

Throughout my college journey, the support I had from home and college allowed me to find myself in a new way. Decision-making became the new accountability. Some decisions were right on point, others not so much. Regardless, each decision taught life lessons, which set a foundation and pushed me to graduate in 2019 with a 3:45 GPA and a bachelor of arts degree in business administration with a concentration in marketing.

What is the greatest lesson learned?
Decision-making is the new accountability, and accountability speaks to my commitment and responsibility.

What advice would you share with first year college student?
Know that what you put into your college experience is what you will get out of it. It is your responsibility to get the best out of the experience. Have a plan, no matter how temporary, so you are not drifting through.

Tyler
Temple University | Class 2019

THE CROSSOVER: FLAME OUT OR FIGURE IT OUT

The "GAP Year" has become a much more popular concept, thanks to Malia Obama, daughter of Barack Obama, 44th President of the U.S., and Michelle Obama. But, it was a foreign concept in my household. I was raised by a young single mother in Brooklyn, New York. And, it was instilled, no it was ingrained in me, that education was the key to unlocking many possibilities. My mother not only talked about getting an education but demonstrated it. For as long as I can remember, she has been pursuing one degree after another. Now, she is working on her doctoral degree. So, for me, not attending college was not an option. But, her example showed me how to figure it out. The first thing on the list to figure out was how to change my scenery from Brooklyn, NY, and change my educational surroundings.

I needed to see, learn, and fellowship with people who looked like me. I wanted to expand my global perspective, and I did not feel I could do that while remaining in New York. I wanted to push myself beyond my norm and my comfort zone. It didn't take a lot for me to decide to attend Morehouse College in Atlanta, GA. This college serves as the mecca for African American men from all over the country. In this sanctuary, I would be seen and heard beyond the norms of just filling a quota. The standards at this institution of higher learning were higher. The work and the professors were much more difficult. Still, I never felt that it was designed to deter my advancement. Rather, it helped me to develop into the best version of myself.

To my surprise, financing college was not a concern. This is not because my mother was handling the bill. It wasn't a concern because I knew the shortfall in scholarships would be filled with student loans. I believe my generation is probably the largest pool of students who must borrow money to complete their education. Even though difficult at times, I strongly believe that the cost of education should not deter anyone from pursuing their college dream. The tangible benefits are beyond priceless.

I uncovered the benefits of college throughout my college journey. The best year in college for me was my freshman year. I gained my wings of independence. I began to dance to the beat of my own drum. This was really the beginning of my life skills. I also considered this time as a crossover to finding myself.

For many African American men, simply enrolling in college is a success story; however, many get lost on arrival, and the question becomes, what's next? My classmates and I found it was easy to flame out, which was our code word for burnout, if we did not figure the steps to take.

For example, my peers and I were the last generation of pre-uber students. Uber was present, but as college students, we could not afford it. So, wherever we went, we had to figure it out, whether on foot, carpooling, or MARTA. NYC Transit is way better. Being a part of the Atlanta University Center (AUC) system and cross-mingling with Clark, Spelman, Georgia Tech, etc., always provided opportunities for excitement and something to do. However, it also forced me to figure out how I should manage it all.

Having a planned schedule was key. Monday through Thursday was for school and homework. Friday and Saturday were, well, you know, the time to get into whatever was good.

It's crucial to be encircled by like-minded people. My friends and I would hang out in the library during the week, so much so that the library staff was sad to see us go in our senior year.

Academically I was prepared from home and high school. However, the social aspect of college life was a little overwhelming. It was in this area that I struggled!

My dating years in high school were limited, primarily for lack of choices. I was looking forward to expanding this in college. To my surprise, what I thought dating was going to be in college would turn out to be completely different. Establishing a relationship was not at the forefront of my mind nor on the minds of my female peers. There was always a conflict between being in a relationship and having a "moment." Thus, I encountered frustration, disappointment, and hurt feelings.

Another area in which I struggled was losing personal space and operating successfully in a confined space. Dormitory life can be fun, but it does not come without some trying situations. For example, living in a dorm, I had to deal with waiting to use the shower, hot water running out, people smoking marijuana, and masturbating in the bathroom; it was just CRAZY! But this was the life I was living, and it was a life to which I had to become accustomed.

Though uncomfortable, I had to get comfortable with being uncomfortable. Think about it, two young men exploring self and life cramped into a 12 by 19 living space. I could not wait to move into my own living space. Until then, I went home as much as possible. All these experiences shaped my college experience and my view of the world.

What helped me through college and after is networking and building relationships. Being a newspaper writer for the school enhanced my social skills tremendously. I connected with anyone I could, a person from a class or someone I would see in the student center; I always felt as if everyone had something to offer. I was intentional in fostering relationships that presented great opportunities and put me in a position to have inside connections to be in important places when others could not. The years flew by, so I appreciated the relationships that I was able to make. I still live with one of my roommates from college today. I graduated with a 3.32 GPA and a bachelor of arts degree in communications. Following graduation, I enrolled in and later graduated from American University with MA in political communications. The person I am today is because I stepped outside of the bubble into uncharted territory. I am grateful!

What is the greatest lesson learned?

It is not what you know; it is who you know! You can be the smartest person in the world. And someone else may know less, but they can take advantage of the same or even better opportunities because they know the right person for the right situation. Treat everyone with respect because you never know when your paths will cross again.

What advice would you share with first year college student?

First, get comfortable with being uncomfortable! Second, get comfortable learning how to maneuver in a new space, environment, people, and challenges. High school may have been easy, but college will not be, but it will shape you for what you desire if you embrace the experience.

Kevin Colclough | Class of 2017
Morehouse College

THE MUSIC BEHIND THE ACADEMICS

I was clear about one thing during my senior year of high school: I did not want to go to college. It was equally clear to my parents that I would not just sit around the house. Nor would I join the military, which was strange coming from two military parents who were honorably discharged and Colonel Majors. So, what was I to do? Peace had to be kept, and a happy medium agreed upon. Thus, I turned my attention to the University of Maryland Eastern Shore. Since this college thing was becoming a reality, I knew I would easily adjust to college from my high school experience because of my love for music and being in the band.

To my surprise, one of my friends unknowingly signed us up for Delaware State University band auditions. She informed me the day before the audition. After the shock wore off, I agreed. How could I not because music was an intricate part of who I am. Not so surprising, I was selected to be a band member. However, I had to shift my focus. I was a percussionist for years, but the offer was contingent upon me playing in the tuba section. So, began my Delaware State University journey, fall 2011. My band experience grounded me quickly to the college experience. My bandmates and director further instilled the skills of discipline, which originated with my military parents. You get the picture! Discipline coupled with patience and scheduling all kept me focused academically.

My college years forced me to grow up quickly. I was now responsible for how and when things got executed and if they were to happen timely. Even though I was growing up, I found time to stay connected to home, which I found to be an essential part of my support system. I did not only call for money; I also wanted my family to understand what I was going through and who I was becoming. I considered myself blessed as I did not have to encounter many of the struggles—financial aid issues to distracting and sometimes debilitating heartbreak, to not integrating into college life well—which I witnessed unfold for so many others. An added benefit was being a member of the band. The experience became even more enriching when I was granted the privilege to join, though not easy, Kappa Kappa Psi in 2013. This new role allowed me to network more, mentor, and help new band members with their college transition. Because of this experience, I was a Charter Founding member of Phi Mu Alpha music fraternity in 2013. Although Phi Mu Alpha was a music Fraternity like Kappa Kappa Psi, it differed in that its goal was to reach the world through the art of music. It also saw music as a bridge, a universal language. In contrast, Kappa Kappa Psi enriched the lives of the band members and forged greater comradery.

With all of the activities I had going on, scheduling and time management were key. My schedule was packed, of course, band, track & field, and so much more. I know I could not actually participate in any of these activities if I did have the grades. My lowest GPA throughout my college journey was 3.20. Every other semester it was a 3.50 and better. I prided myself on my grades, not only for being in the band but for my parents and for myself. Though peculiar to some, a driving thought that helped me stay focused and achieve my grades remained debt-free, and I kept that as a high priority. I knew if I failed any classes, I would be the one responsible for paying to retake them. So, my constant thought was one and done.

Before graduating from Delaware State University, I was again honored to expand my network and join the ranks of some of the phenomenal men. I was invited to join the Divine-9 family through the Gamma Upsilon chapter of Phi Beta Sigma Fraternity, Inc., Spring 2015. This experience further opened my eyes to the mentorship I would now receive from older men. Their focus is cultivating young men to be productive in the world and leave it better than they found it. Phi Beta Sigma Fraternity, Inc. men believe in having a social identity for themselves, others, and the community.

I am pleased to say I graduated in 2015 with a 3.70 GPA and a bachelor of arts degree in criminal justice. I also am a much more well-rounded young man who has learned a great deal from the college experience. However, I know that I have a lot more to learn because learning doesn't end with commencement; it is just beginning.

What is the greatest lesson learned?
I learned to never stop learning and networking. You never know the people who could help impact your future while you're in college. I learned not only to be a student that simply goes to class and back to the dorm room, but rather a student that engages with organizations and prepares for the future.

What advice would you share with first year college student?
Your first year may be the most stressful because you're in a completely new environment. Create a schedule, aligning themselves with their studies first, and then venture into campus activities. Time management will decrease your stress in juggling everything.

James Peteet
Delaware State University | Class of 2015

HIGHER EDUCATION ABCs—ADVOCACY, BALANCE, AND COMMUNICATION

The structure and rigor of high school prepared me for college in more ways than I realized. The importance of preparation was instilled in me by my mother. She was an educator in the New York City Department of Education while I attended LaGuardia Performing Arts High School. There was no time or room in my schedule for anything. Fifty percent (50%) of my schedule was academics, and fifty percent (50%) was performance. Both had to be matched with one hundred percent (100%) intensity. The college conversation had taken place for years in my household. It was much more than a general conversation. Though the choice was mine to make, I was strongly encouraged by my mother and aunties—they know who they are—to attend the illustrious Hampton University, as some may say, the real HU! A family connection provided the opportunity to visit the campus numerous times before I made my final decision. Making the decision was easy because I fell in love with the campus, the people, the vibe, and the city by the sea. I enrolled at Hampton University in Fall 2004.

My preparation from LaGuardia fell a little short on the social aspect of college. Here I was an only child from the big apple—NYC. I was used to my own space, room, and items. Now I had to share a room, which was a lot smaller than my room at home. I started to think, "Oh Lord, how am I going to make it?" One thing that made the transition smoother was connecting with my new roommate before arriving on campus. The college provided basic contact information, and we connected, communicated, and found our commonalities before our arrival - what a relief. In addition to having to adapt to a roommate, there were social and cultural norms that were very different. In New York City, I could go anywhere with a 24-hour NYC transit system. In contrast, things were slower in this new southern culture, and accessibility to everything was reduced drastically.

My mother remained with me the first week of my arrival, and then the world of being an adult began. It was completely nerve-wracking. Yet, attending a Historically Black College and University (HBCU) provided a sense of community. This community was an extension of what I had known and experienced living in New York. For example, each borough in NYC has its own cultural identity and language. The HBCU experience broadened my scope to see black culture on the global scale of the diaspora. It was an exciting lesson. The first year at Hampton was like treading water in so many ways. Losing sight or drowning socially or academically was not an option. By the end of my first year, I had a decent grasp on who to consider friends and associates. I actively took advantage of my professor's office hours. This was important to me because my professor needed to know who I was. I may not have always performed as well as I would have liked, but they knew my level of understanding and effort.

By my sophomore year, being an adult got real, and advocacy was now my responsibility. My built-in backup was gone, or at least was now playing a different role. I had to learn how to advocate for myself and know where the correct resources were to resolve any of the issues I encountered. I had to exercise my voice, present my case, inform authority figures (bursar, etc.) why I thought they were incorrect in their assessment. These were all new and nerve-wracking skills that I had to develop.

As I moved through my college journey, things also got busier, so creating balance was necessary.

I had always been active in dance, track & field, played an instrument; it was important to take the extracurricular mindset with me. So, with my mother's encouragement, I plunged into social life with a bit of trepidation, not wanting to make mistakes but also wanting to have fun. I partied, dated, and visited other college campuses. Soon, I had the privilege to join the ranks of my mother's sorority, Alpha Kappa Alpha Sorority, Incorporated, the Gamma Theta Chapter in 2007. They became the sisters I never had, and I was elated! The experience taught me a lot. I learned more about myself and others. Specifically, I learned how to see others for who they are based on their behavior and not by their words.

During this time, friendships and sisterhood dynamics were tested, which allowed me to be reflective, reevaluate, and redesign expectations for myself and others. In addition, this experience, coupled with my schoolwork and clubs, was a safe place for me to test my multitasking skills effectively and efficiently, which was about primarily maintaining a balance.

I had to realize it was okay not to be okay with people and or situations. What helped in situations like these was communication. Communication was key, in good or bad situations. A perfect example of my college ABCs happened with my roommate during my sophomore year; we clashed on everything; it was a nightmare. My focus was she had to go! I implored, advocated, and communicated but, none of it worked in my favor. Yet another disappointing life lesson was learned-just because I did everything right did not mean that the situation will turn out in my favor. This is something that we see all too often in our society today.

The college years moved swiftly, and my responsibilities grew. First, I had to declare a major. Usually a difficult task for many, however, I was focused and knew my intended area of study—psychology—upon entering Hampton. What was not as clear to me or easy to figure out was which study method would work best for me. I had to learn how to study and retain a vast amount of information. I had to read-reread and reread again, along with utilizing the library. I discovered that isolation worked for me. My professors' office hours became my friend. I could get more acquainted with professors. But to be honest, there were times that I was so embarrassed that I still did not understand the course material. As such, I did not want to take up any more class time with others who appeared to understand. I later learned everyone who said they understood did not!

In my junior and senior years, I found myself, and my confidence increased. I knew it, and others noticed also. It was not a new Stacey, just a more improved version of myself. Graduating from Hampton University, my mother's alma mater, as her soror on Mother's Day weekend 2008 with a Bachelor of Arts in Psychology and a 3.49 GPA was beyond exhilarating.

What is the greatest lesson learned?
Advocacy! The college experience is a system being operated by others. Learn the best way to navigate the system, which translates outside of the college experience to the real world.

What advice would you share with first year college student?
Have fun! Remember to stay balanced. If you allow it to be, it will be everything you want it to be. Stay positive.

Stacey
Hampton University | Class of 2008

DR. VEE'S SEEDS FOR SELF-DISCOVERY

The self-discovery that happens during the college years is often a liberating experience. It is a time when students will assess their identity and the identity they want to develop. This time of discovery shapes who students say they are versus the label the world would ascribe. The self- discovery process is the catalyst to who students will become and how they show up in the world.

What you learn about yourself in self-discovery goes beyond the classroom and self. The discovery will transform students' thinking enabling them to be critical, concerned citizens. Even older students can experience self-discovery and learn new things about themselves as they reconcile new skills into personal and professional development that produces outcomes for a better life. This, after all, is the goal for students of any age.

SECTION 5
FAMILY MATTERS

In the mid-nineties, there was a television show titled Family Matters, also the theme of this section. The show's heart was about the nuclear family and extended family supporting each other to achieve a common goal and make life easier. The college experience is no different, whether it's the family one is born into or having the privilege to pick friends who become family. Family dynamics are essential to the learning process, not only academically but personally.

In 2018, the UK Council on Student Affairs conducted an online study of 1700 students about their perception of the impact of family on their studies and college experience. Of those surveyed, 87% indicated they maintain some form of verbal or non-verbal communication, whether text, facetime, phone calls, etc., at least once a week, if not more. The family connection often aids students in their transition into college life; it fosters an increased sense of belonging, self-belief and decreases personal and academic stress.

Creating a balance between college life and a family is crucial. If family matters overflow into academic life, the results are often detrimental for the student.

Sometimes it is beneficial for students to maintain boundaries with some family members so they can focus on their studies.

These stories highlight how family dynamics and issues impacted their academic journey, fostering a sense of resilience to complete the task not only for themselves but for the family.

A MOTHER'S SACRIFICE

The land of opportunity—The USA. I, an immigrant from West Africa, Ivory Coast, was here in the land of opportunity—The USA—with my growing family. Believing in my heart that there was more to life and education will help me obtain it. I could benefit from this education in the USA and back home also. Education has always been important to me, but back home, there were age restrictions. However, that is not so in the United States of America.

I am a 41-year-old woman graduating with my Associate degree. What I find funny about my college journey is that the focus was not to earn a degree. In 2012, I enrolled in City University of New York (CUNY) LaGuardia Community College because I needed to learn English. English was my ticket to job security. At the time, I had my first child, so I could only work part- time and take classes in the evening. This schedule became increasingly difficult because my husband also worked evenings. Money was tight, and paying for a babysitter was challenging. I also had reservations about babysitters from past experiences in my home country.

In 2014, I eventually found full-time employment as a Therapy-Aid at a psychiatric hospital. I worked until a month before my baby girl arrived in February 2018. Employment had occupied my time, and time waits for no one — years flew by, and I found myself in Fall 2018 still with no degree and now unemployed. I was also concerned about my niece. I encouraged her to attend Bronx Community College in the Spring 2019 semester. She was nervous because she spoke very little English. While I waited with her, I asked myself, what would I need to begin my own college journey? The admission representative was overjoyed; my admission process would be simple being I had previously attended a CUNY college- LaGuardia Community College. All which was required was to pay a $65 application fee, and I was IN. I was too excited! The dream deferred was about to begin, and a new chapter was about to start. The excitement was short- lived. When I got home and informed my husband, he wasn't happy; college was not planned. I guess my focus should have been finding employment and not earning a degree as we had three children to feed and clothe.

We could barely make ends meet, but I wasn't going to be discouraged. God had given me another chance, and I would make this work somehow.

During the first semester, everything was an adjustment. I had to coordinate school and family life. I passed my Test for Adult Basic Education (TABE) test and received full financial aid; this was such a relief. However, the relief was brief. By the second semester, I didn't receive all of my financial aid, and I had a balance of a little over $2000. What in the world! I had no idea how I would pay for this outstanding balance. As a result, I was unable to register for my classes in Spring 2020. I was devastated, and I thought my goal was slipping away. However, I was determined that this would not be the end of my story.

I found a job at Whole Foods. I saved and paid off my school fees and prepared to re-enrolled in Fall 2020. This was a difficult time, and the world as we knew it was on lockdown due to the spreading virus COVID-19. A small part of me was happy that I did not have to attend school in person because all classes went online. I wasn't too familiar with the technology. However, I was focused and pressing forward. The goal was to return to school the following semester. Everything would be back to normal by then, right? NO!

I re-enrolled in Fall 2020. All classes were remote. Here was yet another obstacle. I barely knew how to turn on a computer. Before the shutdown, I had taken two asynchronous classes, and I struggled. I kept missing assignments because I did not know how to locate the assignments or post them. How was I going to survive taking five (5) classes online? Not only was I concerned about passing my classes, but my children were important also. I was now a mother of three children ages 10, 6, and 18-months. There was heartache and dissension in my family when I made the difficult decision to send my precious baby girl back home to West Africa. The baby girl that I always wanted, prayed for, I had to sacrifice and be separated. I would miss many of her firsts. Although I knew it was for a short time and for a bigger purpose, it did not stop my heart from aching daily for her. To say that my family was displeased and sad is an understatement. Our sorrow was compounded when my husband lost his little sister. There was so much going on that it became difficult to think. However, the decision I made was necessary for me to achieve my goal of obtaining my degree.

I was grateful to have found work again, especially since I had another tuition bill hanging over my head for $4600. The 12–14-hour shifts on my job left little time to see my family and complete my schoolwork. The only time I would see my children is when they were sleeping.

My goal to graduate stretches beyond Bronx Community College. I plan to obtain my four-year degree and then build a daycare center back in my country where children can be safe. There is a lot of human trafficking in my country. People will pose as babysitters, and then parents never see their child again.

My sisters back home are educators, too, and are excited to participate in this project. I have learned so much about myself during this journey. There is nothing impossible in the land of possibilities. I will graduate in May of 2021 with my 3.65 grade point average (GPA), and I will enroll in New York University (NYU) or Hunter College. 🎓

What was your greatest lesson?
Success is not promised, but failure is not final; it's the courage to continue that counts.

What advice would you share with first year college student?
Give it your all, do not limit yourself. Explore all college has to offer. You must be passionate about something, and it will carry you through those tough days.

Florence Brou
CUNY- Bronx Community College | Class of 2021

THERE'S NO PLACE LIKE HOME

I was ready to explore a new world after my high school graduation. With that thought in mind, I enrolled in SUNY-University at Albany. The exploration led me to learn that it was not the place for me, even though it was a nice college. The university was too big, and it seemed like each person I encountered had a big personality to fit in as well. I decided I would rather be closer to home and transferred to Mercy College. At Mercy, I was able to find myself. They had a smaller campus and class sizes, so my professors knew who I was. I was able to select a major relative to my intended career aspiration. I definitely enjoyed meeting new people and learning new things from them as well. The new people I met showed me that even though we come from different places, we all go through the same experiences. However, how we view them may be different because of our own beliefs and perspectives.

Once I was in an environment where I felt comfortable, I knew I would continue to thrive in my academics. I always enjoyed learning. My struggle was and has been to overcome my shyness and my introverted nature by talking and opening up to different people. To meet people, network, and find the support I needed and wanted, I had to allow myself to absorb all that college had to offer. So, I participated in charitable activities, such as preparing food baskets for the homeless during Thanksgiving. Doing so opened up a new world for me, and I enjoyed my experience. I set new goals, such as participating in other charitable activities within my school environment and living community. Very rarely was there a semester where I wasn't overwhelmed at one point. However, I would take a step back, breathe, and break down projects or situations one step at a time during those periods. Scheduling, time management became my trusted friend to tackle multiple assignments that were due simultaneously. I would sort out my assignments from least to most intense. I applied a similar strategy during midterms and final exam periods; I would study and go over information from each subject each night to prepare myself. Utilizing strategies like these decreased my anxiety that would often cause me to spiral out of control and not get any work done. Throughout college, I had a great support system from family and friends, who did not let me stay discouraged for too long and helped to redirect my focus.

Gaining my independence was one of the biggest lessons during my college experience. Creating a balance between schoolwork, social activities, and working was not easy. I found celebrating was a stress reliever and aided me in recuperating after a challenging semester. The rewards after an assignment or semester are just as important as completing the assignments and taking the exams. Even though I had family and friends, decision-making rested with me. The decision to return home created a transportation issue for me, which I did not have while I was away. I had to figure out the best way to earn money and save money to continue my education. This was not factored in when I decided to return home. In addition to remaining on top of my schoolwork, I had to set a goal to purchase a vehicle, nothing fancy; it was just to get me from point A to point B. I achieved this goal in a short period—6 months. This made life so much easier.

Being fresh off graduating with my bachelor of science degree with a GPA of 3.8, I am still basking in the accomplishment and looking forward to stepping into a new phase of my life. While I am excited about graduating, I am still anxious about continuing my education and working towards my Master of Science degree in occupational therapy. I do not know what's exactly in store for me. Yet, I know that with my continued support from family and friends and what I've learned through my undergraduate studies, I know it'll all work out in the end.

What is the greatest lesson learned?
Where I was originally was not where I was meant to be. I had to leave what I thought was my first-choice school to grow into who I am today.

What advice would you share with first year college student?
Work hard, stay calm when things look troubling, allow yourself to absorb all the college life has to offer.

M.O.
Mercy College | Class of 2021

IT'S ABOUT THE RIGHT FIT!

I prayed for high school to be over! I attended Edward R. Murrow High School and was not the greatest student because I had some academic challenges and didn't take school seriously. Being a young black man in Brooklyn, New York, attending school was one way to stay out of trouble and off the New York Police Department's radar. For, a black male merely walking down the street can be problematic. Though I had little interest, I enrolled at CUNY-Medgar Evers College in 2014, primarily for proximity. With little guidance, I majored in business administration, a big mistake. I had a desire to own my own business one day but was unsure of the particulars. Unfortunately, a year later, I was no clearer than when I started. The disappointment added to my lack of interest, which was compounded with major family issues, which is not a good combination while attending college.

During the time frame from 2015-2018, my birth mother dealt with major health issues; she had suffered a major stroke. Her health issues plagued my mind daily; it was difficult to concentrate in classes. This subsequently had an adverse effect on my schoolwork and grades. I was worried all the time about what would happen to her. Not a month went by that she wasn't in the hospital for one reason or another, and to make matters worse, I was assigned as her health proxy. The weight of that responsibility was sometimes unbearable. However, I am grateful for friends and family who provided me a village of support along with my therapist. They were a guiding light during very dark times, and for that, I am grateful!

My college journey may appear backward to leave a four-year school and enroll in a two-year community college. However, there is an African proverb that states, "go back to get through." I relate to that because I began my studies at a four-year, transferred to a two-year, graduated, and transferred back to a four-year, but it was all about the fit. The community college setting and overall environment were a better fit for my needs. I am a student with challenges. I was once labeled a special needs student, which required services through special education. But I overcame the challenges. The fit, the support, and the smaller classes all played a vital role in my academic success.

At first, college was good, but I felt like more of a number than a student. My professors rendered their own thoughts, opinions and were not necessarily open to conflicting views (e.g., 9/11). I needed something a little more, personal touch, and I found that at another CUNY at Borough of Manhattan Community college. The financial aspect also was a factor for my transferring. Creating a balance between my personal and school life proved to be an adjustment that I had not dealt with in high school. To be successful, I needed to establish a schedule and find resources to assist me. I was aware enough to know I could not do this on my own.

One of my darkest times during college was when my birth mother died on June 11, 2018. That day will forever be etched into my mind. I remember the day vividly. I was home getting ready for school; for three years, I knew the day would happen. I just did not know how I would respond when it did due to our relationship type. Well, I was not ready for it at all. The type of relationship didn't matter. I was broken. We had created in the later years of her life our own cocoon. She became a soft place for me to land and vent about my professors when the work was too difficult to understand. She lent me her ear even while she battled her body full of pain. I am conflicted with her death; I did not get the opportunity to see her before she died. Lack of planning, I hadn't finished schoolwork, and I put off my visit to her, thinking I still had time later in the week; it wasn't so. I live with that regret, but I take joy in knowing she was proud that I was completing my studies. I've wrestled with "if" I had made the right decision that day about postponing the visit? Did she think I did not care? Those questions and others remain unanswered until today and preoccupied my thoughts so much I had to delay graduation as I took fewer classes to focus and be successful.

On the other side of the conflict, I miss her so much. Her death brought relief because her pain was unbearable for both of us. If I didn't know I needed counseling before, I knew I needed it then. The broken pieces of myself needed to be put back together, and I had to make sense of it all; death and college are not a good combination.

Though difficult, my mothers' death provided a restart. Through playing basketball, I released stress, found new friends and outlets at the college; I joined the Teacher Education Club. This experience provided new insights into my new major, Elementary Education. I networked within the club, and my professors gave me the additional support I had lost due to my mother's death.

Though the journey has been long, I graduated with an associate's degree in early childhood education and a 2.20 GPA. I found the right four-year university fit at CUNY-City College, pursuing a bachelor's degree in childhood education.

What is the greatest lesson learned?
Finding and creating a balance between all the essential things in life (personal, social, and academic). I can overcome any obstacles as long as I remain focused.

What advice would you share with first year college student?
Don't let labels define you, special education or otherwise. Also, don't carry the limitations others place on you; it's too heavy. If you require extra support, ask for it! If I can succeed in college having a background in special education, so can you. Lastly, find a balance and have fun while completing your studies.

Anthony
CUNY-Borough of Manhattan Community College | Class of 2020

ALL IN THE FAMILY

Attending college was always a goal of mine. I knew that not only would I attend and graduate, as the years progressed, I would further my education. For many, attending college is connected to achieving a certain income potential. It was no different for me; especially being a minority, it was instilled in me that the only way to succeed is to receive as many degrees as possible. Looking back at it, I don't think that getting an education will guarantee me decent pay in the future, but it can only increase my chances. The real driving force to attending college was my family and a deep desire to learn, be well educated, and impact society. I had a decent amount of college choices; however, 'Cuse', as often referenced, was the right fit. I chose to attend Syracuse University at the time because that was the only school that truly aligned with what I thought I wanted in a school. An equally important factor was that it was one of the only schools that offered me a pretty decent financial aid package. If not for those reasons, I believe I would have attended another school and probably out of state.

Though I wish I had more positive experiences during my time at Syracuse, I truly enjoyed the people and relationships I formed with my friends. I now consider my family. Relationship building is essential! These friendships turned into something deeper because we all went through hard times together, but we always supported and lifted each other up through those hard times. Though there were challenging times, I believe I was meant to be at Syracuse for those reasons alone.

In addition, there was something about being a minority at a predominantly white institution (PWI) that, I believe, fortified my relationship with other students of color. I don't think I would have had that with peers at another college. We endured together, which made our bond stronger, forming that familial aspect we now have. This internal village helped shape my experience and served as insulation from some of the harsh realities that I and many other minorities face in a sea of a 40,000 students.

Being away from home was nothing new for me. I had attended boarding school for my high school studies. However, venturing out beyond the borders of the United States of America to study was the highlight of my college experience. My horizon was expanding academically, emotionally, and personally as I spent a semester abroad in London, UK. My time abroad was a huge learning experience. I was stretched out of my comfort zone, but I enjoyed it. I learned the depths of my capabilities as a student and my strengths and capabilities as a Black woman in this world. I was able to see up close and personal the global perspective of education and being a black woman. There did not appear to be much difference on the surface, but when you looked closer, it was there. I noticed it through the curriculum, which I had to learn how to manage, the community I lived in, and the places I traveled to. The experience alone helped me blossom as an individual, and it propelled me to advocate for minority students to experience study-abroad opportunities. Many students miss the opportunity because they believe the study-board option is too expensive. However, completed during the school semester, in most cases, your financial aid will cover the cost. I was lucky enough to have an advisor who was a person of color. She believed in me and helped me to navigate the study abroad process. I will forever be grateful for him and that study abroad experience.

Mental stamina is real! And it was one of the biggest challenges I had to overcome to finish college without burning myself out completely. The thought that college is all fun, games, and partying, can quickly spiral you out of control. It is hard academically and mentally. The mental challenges are often not spoken about in the college experience. There were days when, mentally, I just had no energy to go to class. Especially in the winter when it snowed a lot, I found every reason I possibly could to avoid going to class. In those moments, I reminded myself of my purpose, goals, and ideals, and I found a way to get my work done. The work wasn't always perfect, and I didn't always get As, but that's perfectly fine because I did what I needed to get my degree and move on to the next stage in life. As my college years went on, I became more intentional with my self-care and mental health. I made sure to schedule time every week to do something for myself that took me away mentally and physically from school and assignments. The things I did for myself included making dinner, watching tv with my roommates, washing my hair, changing my room around, and working out, for example. These may appear small, but they had a huge impact and kept me going in the end.

In my senior year of college, I also made sure to spend time with my friends as our time was short, and we would be going our separate ways. This was possible because I intentionally created my schedule to have the least number of classes by my senior year. And those classes would not be challenging.

I had looked forward to this moment; graduation was an exciting time for me. I did it for me but also for my mom and dad. Neither of them had graduated from college. They had sacrificed for my sister and me. When COVID-19 turned our world upside, I was devastated for many reasons, especially about not participating in traditional graduation. Internally I felt robbed, like I did not really finish.

I had the summer, and then I began my studies for my master's degree in forensic psychology. My mind felt like it was on a regular summer break, not a transition into another stage of adulthood. However, I am grateful to have been accepted into my graduate program before a pandemic. It was an achievement for me and reminded me that I still know what my purpose is. The pandemic changed how I view learning and school; it puts things into perspective on how things can change instantly and how we as a people must be adaptable for survival. Being able to adapt to anything thrown your way is vital for college but for life as well.

What is the greatest lesson learned?
Plans change; we change, don't get stuck in your thinking, be comfortable with adapting to change.

What advice would you share with first year college student?
Be adaptable and know it is fine to not have all the answers for school or life.

Aleyah
Syracuse University | Class of 2020

AND 5-6-7-8—IT'S THE 8-COUNT FOR ME!

The count of ". . . and 5-6-7-8!"was always to kick-start for me, and my education was no different. My education has always been the first priority in my life, and it was encouraged by my mom. I knew about the weight education held in the real world. Unfortunately, finances are one of the prime factors for the decrease in college enrollment. When my mom got sick with breast cancer for the third time, I was in high school, and I knew that I had to apply for more scholarships than the average junior student. Although I was stepping into young adulthood, I was still a child, and I did not want my mother to worry about my college tuition. She had larger-than-life issues to contend with, from her treatment for cancer to massive medical expenses. My mother, my biggest supporter, constantly encouraged me while she was going through treatment.

She pushed me to stay focused and to prepare for college. So, not only did I work hard to make her proud but to prove something to myself. I signed up for college tours and auditioned for the dance and acting programs of my choice.

There is an old adage that God is never late; HE is always right on time. I was blessed and given the opportunity of a lifetime and received the Gates Millennium Scholarship funded by Bill and Melinda Gates. This scholarship is for minorities, and the program pays for tuition up to a doctoral degree. I was elated when I got the news that I had received this life-changing scholarship. In fact, as soon as I found out, I knew exactly what school I wanted to attend Virginia Commonwealth University's (VCU) for dance. When I visited VCU, I instantly fell in love with the campus and its dance program. The teachers were welcoming, and it seemed like the perfect family-oriented environment that every student yearns for when attending college. Also, in high school, I never had the full experience of going to pep rallies and basketball games because my high school was strictly arts-based. We had our academic schedule from 8 a.m. to 2 p.m., and from 2 p.m. to 5 p.m., we had our arts major schedule. I felt as if I was in a 9 to 5 job, but it was excellent preparation for the real world. For this reason, VCU was the perfect blend of offering me a warm experience and an amazing dance training program, and educational wealth.

I couldn't picture myself anywhere else other than at VCU as an undergraduate. My teachers were driven, compassionate, personable, intelligent, and overall incredible. I can honestly say I've learned so many skills in the classroom in college that actually apply to my life now. So, while I experienced my dream college experience, I got a quick life lesson. Life is not always as it seems. During my sophomore year, my mom was diagnosed with a rare incurable autoimmune condition known as Mixed Connective Tissue Disease. She also had other conditions that negatively affected her health. During this challenging time, my teachers and peers in the dance department were my rocks.

I was in a very dark and depressing space, knowing I was away from my mom and unable to physically help her in any way. I felt lost! I had more questions than answers. I stopped going to class on some days to stay in bed, and on other days, I just broke down in tears in the middle of class. Through it all, dance and the support of my dance community lifted me out of the dark place I had slipped into and brought me back into the light. Without their love and support, I know I would have continued to fall down a hole I knew that I would not be able to escape on my own. I've always been an individual that wanted to figure everything out on my own, but I knew I needed guidance to refrain from falling in the cracks. So, my professors advised me to get involved in some extracurricular activities both outside and inside the dance department to help take my mind off my mother's health conditions. So, I joined a two-year leadership program to help cultivate my leadership/collaboration skills and the Miss Black and Gold Pageant to focus on myself and cheer up my spirits. I also took more time out of my schedule to go to the library for study groups so I could be around more people.

Moreover, another challenge during college was dance itself. Ballet was a weakness. It had always been an area in which I had to work three times as hard as anyone else. My goal has always been to be the dancer I knew that I was capable of being. So, after class was over, I asked my teachers how I could improve my technique. After I received my notes, I spent many hours in the studio practicing so that I could progress in class. Overall, my commitment to overcoming my depression and reaching my academic goals were some of my greatest accomplishments in college. Another achievement I am proud of is my senior capstone project. This project was the first time I choreographed an 11-minute-long piece and auditioned dancers that fit the aesthetic of my storyline. It took me a while to figure out how I would bring my story alive through movement. It consisted of late-night calls with my mom along with reflective moments; it ultimately was the key to unlocking my creative block. All things considered, my piece turned out beautifully and the audience connected with it, which was exactly what I wanted. Despite every challenge, I was able to face the process. My senior project was the final step to the end of my undergraduate journey, and I needed it to be a success. I was proud of myself and everything that I had accomplished during my years in college, and I was excited to graduate. I felt ready to conquer the world and knock over more roadblocks that got in my way.

Shortly after I graduated, things immediately felt different. At the time, I wasn't sure if this was good or bad, but I knew I didn't like the confusion. As usual, I went to my go-to, my mom; after a long in-depth talk with her, I realized it was the atmosphere change and my new schedule structure that suddenly shifted. I was now in the real world; I had real full-time work responsibilities and bills to pay. I instantly missed my friends and everything I had grown to love over those four years. Despite missing school, I can honestly say that I am thankful for my undergraduate college experience. I learned how crucial building relationships and networking can be. I also learned to never take any experience for granted.

What is the greatest lesson learned?
The most important lesson I learned while in college is that it is okay to ask for help. We are human, and having a support system in your corner is critical, especially during hard times.

What advice would you share with first year college student?
It is okay to make mistakes. It is also important to make friends, step out of your comfort zone and strive to accomplish every goal you have set for yourself. As students, we owe it to ourselves to have fun and live life to the fullest while not forgetting the meaning of hard work.

Cydney Hill
Virginia Commonwealth University | Class 2019

DR. VEE'S SEEDS FOR THE FAMILY MATTERS

Your life will never be the same and that is a great thing! Whether a student commutes or dorms college is a life-transforming experience for not only the student attending college but the family too. An adjustment is essential for all members of the family. Whether the college student is the traditional 18-year-old student or the non-traditional 24 years working student; family dynamics change.

Oftentimes family members will feel that a new person has emerged from the experience. Which is fine! Allow time for the family, parents, siblings, spouses, children to adjust and get to know the new you, invite them into this new world, new ideas, and new people you have encountered. Celebrate with your family as it was their support that contributed to the journey.

SECTION 6
NON-TRADITIONAL STUDENTS

It's never too late to experience college and all that it has to offer. The college journey is something all should experience if they so desire. Time nor age should not be a determining factor. This has been most evident in the past few decades.

The U.S. Department of Education reports that there has been a 15 percent increase in non-traditional students returning to the halls of academia. A non-traditional student is someone who did not attend and complete college right out of high school and is older than a traditional-aged college student (18-24). Whether a non-traditional student decides to satisfy a personal goal, reaches a career obligation for promotion, or completes unfinished business, non-traditional students must understand there is a space and place for them.

Colleges and universities across the country are taking strides to accommodate and meet the needs of this population. Many non-traditional students have a vast amount of life experience and obligations than their younger, traditional counterparts. Thus, the need for flexibility of courses, online classes, and a sense of community in addition to their families. Non-traditional students, as of late, are finding extraordinary value in their decision to return to the classroom.

These stories highlight the sacrifices, the dilemmas, and the balancing acts many non-traditional students encounter. However, they forge through to cross the finish line and onto the graduation stage.

THE BREAKS DID NOT BREAK ME!

Where do I start? I was broken in ways that were not even clear to me. The brokenness manifested in my behavior. I was a troubled teenager. I barely graduated from Poughkeepsie High School with a 65 grade point average. Luckily, I found a college SUNY-Old Westbury, New York that would take me. This was the summer of 1998. I enrolled reluctantly, but it was a lifesaver. I experienced freedom from home life and escape from trouble, or so I thought. My next saving grace was a United States Army Military Recruiter. I was looking at a possible three-year jail sentence, so the military sounded like a wonderful idea, and it actually was.

In 1999, while in the military that I began to find myself. I began to break the confusion around who I was and what I wanted. I was dealing with a cultural clash. I was a Jamaican, supplanted in the United States, experiencing a gender identity crisis along with a desire to be rough and tough. All of this while still trying to meet family expectations of femininity with skirts and dresses. Oh, what a confusing time! My confusion had been expressed in my earlier behavior, but I found purpose as a soldier in the military. Could there be a thing of finding too much purpose in a mission? Maybe- for me, I placed the mission over marriage, two divorces, and delayed the growth of my family with terminating a pregnancy- all for the mission. Now the mission was not just the U.S. military. The mission was financial security, and nothing was going to stop me -well, once again, so I thought.

There were numerous breaks in my college journey, but it always remained a nagging thought. After getting settled in the military, I figured I would enroll in college again. The time was 2004, Chapman University-California. It was a short stint, but I managed to earn a few more credits. At this time, there was a shift; I had decided to join the New York Army National Guard, which required me to have a full-time civilian job. I was so internally connected to the military I had to find something which paralleled military ideology. This led me to the Federal Correction System in 2005. Reality hit! Here I was, with a full-time job and the responsibility of being a mother. I had given birth to a son the day before 9/11. I began to realize that opportunities were passing me by because I had not completed the mission of a college degree. So, I enrolled in college yet again, this time at Thomas Aquinas College. But, it wasn't long before I was called to duty for another deployment in 2006. However, this time I was determined.

After deployment, I re-enrolled in college in 2008, only to be deployed again in 2011, but this time my deployment was life-changing; I sustained a lower back injury. It was an injury that could change the trajectory of my military career and my life. I was medically evacuated to the hospital unconscious, only to be awakened by having morphine and steroids pumped in me. All the while, I was being informed that I would not walk again. WHAT! I laid in bed, frightened not only for myself but my family and my babies. What would all this mean? I was paralyzed for three days, but through the power of a praying mother and my own determination, I started to have movement in my limbs. I had conquered one hurdle only to be informed that the life I knew in the military was coming to an end due to my injury. I became plagued with depression, anxiety, and PTSD, but I knew there was more for me to do.

I worked hard and focused on things other than myself and earned a medical clearance to deploy one last time for the War in Afghanistan. This mission helped to better secure my family's financial future; however, opportunities continued to escape me because I had not completed my college studies. I returned to St. Thomas Aquinas in 2016 more determined than ever, and this time it paid off. The level of satisfaction I felt in graduating in the middle of a pandemic transformed my world, and the feelings are beyond description.

I am a full-time employee and single mother of three children, and I didn't let anything get in the way of reaching my goal. I am proud to say I graduated with a 3.9 GPA Magna Cum Laude with a bachelor's degree in business administration and a minor in psychology in May 2020. My plans are to get a master's degree in an area yet to be determined.

What is the greatest lesson?
Believe in yourself, and do not discount any part of your life because all the pieces make up the puzzle.

What would you share with a freshman?
You can't finish if you don't start. Be prepared for change. It will come, and your success will be determined by how you handle it.

Ret SSG Ingram, Andrea (US ARMY)
St. Thomas Aquinas College | Class of 2020

MONEY WILL DRIVE YOU, BUT EDUCATION WILL KEEP YOU

Queens, NY, born and raised! I loved Queens, but I also was ready for a change. My educational journey had its fair share of starts and stops, which began as early as elementary to high school. I started school in the NYC public school system and then transferred to St. John's Prep High School, a catholic and predominately White school. Less than 10% of the student population were African American, and those were usually student-athletes. I played basketball, and I was good! I was being recruited, and various scouts had come to see me play. A recruiter from a Division I school, the University of Vermont, was interested. So was I, not because of the school, because I would probably be in the same situation as high school, limited African Americans. However, I knew Division I ball would offer me a scholarship. Unfortunately, I didn't get an opportunity to visit, but my sister shared insightful information since she attended Windham College. I was the number two choice, and the number one had decided to attend Vermont, so I was left without a school. I had to come up with a plan B quickly. College attendance was a must. It was instilled in me by both of my parents, especially my father, a very proud man who took care of his family, was exceptionally skilled in all trades, and was the building Superintendent, Community Organizer, but could not read or write. He did not want the same fate for any of his children to go through life as he did.

So, I moved on to Plan-B, that is, find a new college to call home! I received an impromptu invitation from a friend, who had already received an acceptance letter, to take a ride down to Winston-Salem. I knew my mother's side of the family was from there, making it even more exciting to visit family, including a long-lost brother I didn't know. I arrived at Winston-Salem State University for a week-long orientation. I lost my mind seeing the sea of beautiful people of color- I had found my home!

I sent my basketball tapes to Head Coach Clarence "Big House" Gaines (Naismith Basketball Hall of Famer) and hoped for the best. Winston-Salem is a Division II school, and they didn't give out scholarships like the Division I schools. I enrolled in the Fall of 1985 and brought my New York swag to the south, my three-finger rings, chains, my nickname was Gucci because I always had a Gucci pouch in hand. I made a name for myself quickly and thought it would carry over to basketball. To my surprise, Coach Gaines called me to say, "New York," that's what he called me, "You didn't make the cut to be on the team!" He went on to say that he wanted me to be a practice player. I couldn't believe what I was hearing. Did he know who I was? I came home on break and contemplated transferring, but I wasn't ready to let go of the home away from home college life experience. I returned and played intramural basketball and focused on my studies.

At the beginning of my sophomore year, while heading back to school, I received the most devastating phone call; my father had transitioned, and my mother insisted that I not return home for his services. I think she was concerned I would not complete college. It was a problematic directive to follow, but I did. I slowly began to work more than I studied, and by my junior year, I was making good money and only attended school part-time. Tuition was manageable because I had established myself as a North Carolina resident for in-state tuition by then. The more I worked, the less I attended school. I started working at a Greensboro Airport Marriott and eventually moved back home to work at the Times Square location. I made excellent money, had great connections with athletics and celebrities, and school was not on my radar.

Life continued, I was honored to be accepted to membership into Phi Beta Sigma Fraternity Inc., Epsilon Sigma Chapter (Harlem, New York). It was here that school became a front and center focus again. Most of the brothers had earned their degrees and even had advanced degrees. Here I was mentoring a group of young men ages 8-18, promoting education, and I hadn't completed my degree. Through the inspiration of the brotherhood and my current wife, I returned to college. She had her degree; we supported our son, who was exploring college, and I refused to be the only one without a degree. I enrolled in The College of New Rochelle, Harlem campus in 2016 and studied psychology.

During the last year of my college journey, there were so many distractions that, at another time in my life, they might have derailed me, but my family was extremely supportive. The Harlem campus abruptly closed in 2018, I had to take classes at the Bronx campus, and the entire college closed in 2019. With all these last-minute disruptions, I felt lost and disconnected; I was in my last semester, I could see the finish line. I was determined to do whatever was necessary to complete the journey. That meant attending Mercy College. They had temporarily taken over a few of the campuses to allow graduating seniors to finish. It was a very stressful time.

March 2020, with the introduction of a new normal, quarantine, masks, 6-feet apart, schools were temporarily closed and moved to remote learning.

Yet, another disruption, would this delay what I could feel in my grasp? The completion of this degree was not just for me. It was for so many others, my family and my parents. My father had always said he wanted to live to see me graduate. So, I dedicated my degree to both of my parents.

For a while, I was chasing the paper with the dead presidents instead of chasing the paper (degree) to help me continue to earn the paper with the dead presidents. If I had done things differently, my mother might have seen me graduate. I am beyond proud that all members of my household hold a degree. One week before my son's graduation, I graduated from Mercy college in the middle of the COVID-19 pandemic with a bachelor of arts degree in psychology with a 3.8 GPA. The next paper I am chasing is my masters degree in business administration from Mississippi Valley State University, graduation loading for 2022.

What is the greatest lesson learned?
The conversation changes in the room when you have a degree. It gave me a voice in the room to be heard.

What advice would you share with first year college student?
Don't stop. Think of your journey in terms of six years, not four, go on to earn your masters. Attending an HBCU is a life experience; you will feel like family.

Kevin "K.B." Bracey
Mercy College | Class of 2020

IT'S A DIFFERENT WORLD

I was excited about many things my senior year of high school, one being I would attend an HBCU, a Historically Black College and University. This was important because I had attended and graduated from a predominantly white high school; so, yes, I was excited about having a school experience similar to the show "It's A Different World" (1987-1993). I was going to be around people who looked like me. I was 18 years of age and ready to go! Although I was interested, my actions showed I was not invested or prepared.

I was beyond excited to get my acceptance letter to Virginia Union University in 1993. I didn't understand all which will be required of me in college. I had no real concept of accountability, how to manage my time, how to study. I majored in socializing, parting, basketball games, and the student center, etc. I had no decent grades to speak of and, by the end of the second year, the second semester, I was pregnant. I was scared! What was I going to do? How could I tell my mother? I was grateful after her disappointment wore off; my mother has been my biggest supporter. I had my son! Stayed home and was doing well, so I thought. I was working in the restaurant industry. I wasn't overly concerned with going back to college because I attended The New York Restaurant School (1997-98) and obtained certification. I was good, right!? Nope, 9/11 happened and devastated the restaurant industry in New York; subsequently, I worked dead-end jobs after dead-end jobs.

Years passed, and I eventually landed a part-time job at the New York City Department of Education. My union, DC-37, offered to pay for their employees to attend college. In 2007, I enrolled in The College of New Rochelle. Unbeknown to me, I didn't have any credits worth transferring, so I started my college journey from scratch. This became a teachable moment to get me focused on tackling this journey for the second time.

I had squandered the opportunity to enjoy all the typical pleasures of college life. And now, I had more responsibilities. I had to figure out how to balance motherhood, full-time college, and a part-time job; oh, it was definitely a different world.

Scheduling became my best friend. There was so much work for those 6-credit classes, so much reading and writing; failure was not an option—my son watching me. Going back to college as an adult was challenging. The workload seemed more intense. My professors were younger than me. Imposter syndrome, a collection of feelings of inadequacy that persist despite evident success, forever lingered. With imposter syndrome, the affected individual suffers from chronic self-doubt and a sense of intellectual fraudulence that overrides any feelings of success or external proof of their competence.

One of the things which helped me deal with my internal struggle of imposter syndrome was having peers who were also non-traditional students. Most of us all worked during the day, had family, children, spouses. So, we supported each other. We became a village to each other.

The support was critical as I often felt guilty about the time I could not spend with my son. I instilled in my son the importance of not abusing opportunities and taking full advantage of them when presented; so, you won't to have to play catch up like myself.

The village was also necessary; we had some very tough professors who did not let us have it easy. Whether we were older, doing this the second time, had a family, or working, they all pushed us to rise to the occasion. At the time, I was not happy, but now I very much appreciate it. And as such, I eventually began to have thoughts beyond the bachelor's degree.

My college journey happened just as it was supposed to, derailments and all. I was beaming with excitement when I graduated with my son again, still watching me in June 2011. I continued my educational pursuits and earned a master's degree in June 2014 and a doctoral degree loading… for June 2022.

What is the greatest lesson learned?
One of the greatest lessons that I have learned is to listen and be patient with yourself. I made my life a lot more difficult than it needed to be because I decided that I knew better than all of the adults in my life. We can learn a lot from those who came before us; take time to listen.

I also learned about the importance of education, especially as a young parent. My education has propelled me into settings that I never knew I could enter. I've led conversations where I am the expert sharing my thoughts and lived experiences. Being an educated Black woman ROCKS! I am so grateful to have obtained it because it can never be taken from me.

What advice would you share with first year college student?
Do not be afraid to ask for help. Whether you need help with time management or struggling in a class, ask for help. There are systems in place on all college campuses that are there to assist you. From tutoring centers to counseling centers, support is available to you. You may find that you are more comfortable confiding in one of your professors. If that is the case, have a conversation with your professor and explore a mentoring relationship with them. Remember, college is an adjustment on all levels. It is okay to seek support. You will never know if you never ask.

Kimberly Colclough
The College of New Rochelle | Class 2015

LET'S GET CLEAR!

The very first time I attended college it was 1980, and I was 18 years-old. Attending college was the standard rule in my house. The problem, though, was I had no idea what I wanted to study. I wanted to be an airline stewardess. I know I'm dating myself, but that was my goal at the time, and I figured they would train me to do what was needed. When that did not work out, I was off to college, still confused, but I enrolled at New York City Technical College in Brooklyn. Being guided by my older sister, I took business classes, secretarial, shorthand, those skills which would ensure I always had a job.

Unfortunately, I didn't graduate in 1983 because I was on academic probation. I could not grasp the math classes. I did not think or even know how to get a tutor or to ask for help. I knew that I could not go home without a plan. I dropped out and got a job at Abraham & Straus. Life rolled on, and, in 2003, I was diagnosed with Lupus; from 2003-2007, I struggled with this autoimmune disease and finding the best methods to manage it. It was doctors versus natural medicine. In the middle of this ordeal, approximately twenty years later (2005), I enrolled in Nyack College reluctantly. With my husband's encouragement, I figured this time it would be different.

I was different. This time, I wanted to have a degree, but still, I had no concrete vision for myself. And, by this time, I am a wife and a mother of two girls who were five and seven years of age. Frustration and confusion swirled in my head regularly. How would I go back to school with no extended family or money to pay for college? I did not know what my passion or gifts were. I was just starting to discover them.

I chose Nyack College because of its proximity to my job, and it was a Christian college. I like to understand why people behave in a certain way, so I chose psychology as my major. While attending a traditional college, I became certified as a Licensed Naturopath in 2008. At the same time, my Lupus was deemed inactive.

The adjustment and challenges were more than I could have imagined. Commuting at night, not getting home until 10 p.m. or later, depending on the bus, was stressful. Staying awake in class was a huge challenge. Working all day and sitting in class while a professor lectured was boring! Finding time to do my homework and still creating time for my children, husband, home, and the church was exhausting.

I took a year off to assess my situation and myself mentally. I went back in 2008. I realized I had to change my mindset. In the beginning, I felt as if going to college was a waste of time, especially when a professor would come in and tell you their life story or how they did not get any sleep the night before. I felt like, "Who cares?" and I could not believe that my money was paying for this nonsense. It was not until I had reached the halfway mark in accumulating credits that I felt like I could not stop now. I could not drop out like I did the first time.

Even though it was a constant thought, I would dress in comfortable layers due to my fear of being attacked at night; the layers were a form of protection. My thought was to make it difficult if I was attacked and raped. I was always prepared, I had on comfortable shoes in case I had to run, and I carried a backpack so my hands could be free. This was the constant mental state that I found myself in. Be ready to flee and stay alert became my daily motto. Staying focused for my safety was equally as exhausting as attending classes.

Financing college was an issue. With no real guidance, I took out loans every semester. I had no time or money to waste but remaining focused after a full day of employment was not an easy feat. After a mediocre year of C grades, an adjustment had to be made. I sought permission from my employer to take an extended lunch to take classes and stay after-hours to make up for the shortfall. This also helped with the mental strain of worrying about being attacked. It took me forever to finish. Every semester I wanted to quit. I was an adult surrounded primarily by teenagers or young adults living at home with their parents, and going to school was their life. I did not have their freedom. Every moment was precious. I read and did homework on the bus and at my children's rehearsals. The library served a two-fold purpose for my girls to complete their projects with assistants and for me to do schoolwork. To finish what I had begun, I had several tutors outside of school. Oh yeah, forgot to mention that my husband and I were both in college at the same time. He went during the day and worked a full-time job at night. Insanity! I was able to get his feedback regarding professors and use his books; therefore, I did not have to buy any. That saved a few dollars. "Teamwork makes the dream work," they say, and it did!

Not by choice, but the last year and a half, my classes were only offered online. Though I did not like this format, it freed up my commuting time and became the world we live in since COVID-19. Then it was a huge adjustment because I preferred asking questions and getting a response right away. I wanted the professor to see my face and know that I did not understand what was going on. The stress of group work, a slow-moving computer, losing data because I forgot to save often made me want to scream! Through it all, I am grateful for the support of my husband and God.

We all have milestone occasions, and 2014 was one of them for me. I was finally done! I had stayed the course (2 Tim 4:7). I wanted to continue my studies but refused to accumulate more debt, and I felt it was my girls' time. They were both getting ready to graduate high school and beginning their own college journey. I heard them. They needed more of me as they embarked into this new world. I showed my girls how to stay the course and graduated with a bachelor's degree in Psychology with a 3.25 GPA.

What is the greatest lesson learned?
I am capable of finishing what I started. The degree was for me. I am only considered a failure if I never try. A closed mouth doesn't get fed, so I open my mouth to get what I need and want.

What advice would you share with a college freshman?
Finish it when you're young. The college experience is a life experience. And, life's lessons are priceless. Look for as many scholarships as possible; money is waiting for you. Debt and college do not have to be synonymous. Have the following qualities: Commitment, Learn, Enthusiasm, Ask, Resilient = CLEAR. Be committed to bringing your best, and do not try to be something you are not.

Learn all that you can about yourself and those around you, have an Enthusiasm about new things. Ask for help, ask questions, and resiliency will assist you in recovering from those difficult moments and situations.

Cherise Canton
Nyack College | Class of 2014

REUNITED WITH MY FIRST LOVE ONLINE

Nothing about my college experience was traditional. I graduated from high school in 1980. Moving during the middle of my senior year did not help matters. I did not sign up to take the ACT or SAT. During my junior year of high school, my Creative English teacher sparked an interest in majoring in journalism. After relocating from Florida to Alabama, there was no push from my parents or my teachers in Alabama to enroll in college. I could not totally blame the teachers; they didn't know me, and I only attended class three hours a day. I only needed one credit to graduate. I accepted a job offer and went to work the day after high school graduation. College was a mere thought, always at the back of my mind, of something I would do eventually. I worked full-time, and in 1984 I relocated to Washington, DC.

At 27, I enrolled as a part-time student at the University of the District of Columbia (UDC). My major of interest had not changed, and to become a journalist, would require me to adjust my life for classes on campus. As a budding journalist, I spent time writing and taking photos for the school paper, slowly working my way to the editor. I was invited to join the sisterhood of Sigma Gamma Rho Sorority, Inc., Beta Chapter, after attending an informational meet and greet.

I had recently lost my grandmother, and joining the sorority gave me a sense of sisterhood and purpose. The dilemma I faced at UDC was the required internships, which meant me relinquishing my full-time job. My brothers had recently moved to Washington, DC; the youngest enrolled at UDC and the oldest just completing his college career. I did not want to disrupt my youngest brother's goal, and the older brother was finding work. So, I quit with one hundred quarter hours completed, thirty-six credits shy of receiving a bachelor's degree. Years went by before college became a priority again.

In 2006, now 43 years old, a wife and mother to a toddler, I was determined to finish a goal I started.

It was important for my son to see that he can set a goal and achieve it no matter the age. Only this time, enrolled at the University of Maryland University College (UMUC), I was registered as a part-time student attending online. Initially, my goal was to pursue a degree in Information Technology, as I had spent most of my adult career working in the field. After several attempts to get through the first required coding class, I changed my major to my first love, communication studies, with a concentration in journalism.

The requirement to intern was not a requirement to graduate. After six grueling years of late nights, term papers, praying feverishly to pass College Algebra and Chemistry in 2012, I graduated. I was 49.

It wasn't the best GPA, 2.86, but I was proud. I did not miss one PTA meeting or any of my son's extracurricular activities.

During this stint of getting my undergraduate, another instructor sparked an interest in continuing and thinking about teaching. Taking a semester off, I was ready to tackle a master's program. At least I thought I was. Realizing that I was not going to adjust to the rigid schedule for UMUC's graduate program, I enrolled at Walden University in 2013. Again, I took the virtual route. In 2015, at age 52, I completed all of my requirements to receive another degree, MS in education with a 3.32 GPA.

I cannot say the road traveled was easy. It was stressful, strenuous, and grueling.

There were many nights I barely made the deadline of getting assignments and term papers uploaded. There were tears when things didn't go right and times I wanted to quit. Going to school in a completely virtual environment requires dedication, time management, and reliable internet and computer equipment. Each professor had specific requirements on how they wanted assignments, posts, and papers to look, so I had a different learning curve each semester. It became more manageable when I realized I needed to be flexible each and every term.

Every semester I finished from undergraduate to graduate, I celebrated. I was one step closer to fulfilling my promise to myself. Each step I took, my son watched. I wanted him to see and remember my resilience, determination not to quit, and not giving up.

When I graduated from UMUC with a bachelor of arts degree in communication, my father gifted me a Walt Disney World celebration. At that moment, I did not know who was happier, my father or me. Even though I was the last of my siblings to receive my college degree, I was filled with pride. A lifetime goal completed. All three of us achieved what our parents and grandparents had not, a college degree. The realization for me was seeing my accomplishment through my son's eyes. The promise that I made to that seventeen-year-old high school graduate came true. My dream eventually became my reality. I did it! 🎓

What is the greatest lesson learned?
Despite the obstacles and turns, I took in life, and I completed the goal.

What advice would you share with first year college student?
Remember to breathe when things get demanding. Surround yourself with like-minded individuals who will support your efforts, dreams, and goals.

Lisa Jones Harwell
University of Maryland University College | Class of 2012

DR. VEE'S SEEDS
FOR THE NON-TRADITIONAL STUDENT

The road may have been different and possibly even rough for the nontraditional student, but many have earned a Ph.D. in life experiences. And, with that experience, they bring an unprecedented amount of wealth to classroom learning. Knowing that they are valued based on what they bring to the table increases the rate of academic success and fosters a sense of belonging. The college experience should reflect society as a whole.

Encouraging and embracing different cultures, ages, and levels of education is all part of the learning process and sends a clear message that all are welcome. This is diversity, equity and inclusion at its best!

SECTION 7
BUILDING BLOCKS OF ACADEMIC SUCCESS SKILLS
WIDELY USED RESOURCES IN HIGHER EDUCATION

ACADEMIC SUCCESS SKILLS

Academic
Always keep your GPA above a 2.0 on a 4.0 scale and 1.5 on a 3.0 scale. Failure to comply will have an adverse impact on your financial aid.

College Catalog
This outlines pertinent information about admission, academic requirements, course descriptions, curriculum outlines, how to remain in good standing, and so much more.

Academic Writing
This form of writing is different from everyday writing. It involves research, evaluating, referencing, and analyzing, etc.

Drop Date
This date is key. It indicates when a student can drop a course without any academic penalty; Develop a relationship with your Professors and Academic Advisors.

Essay Exam
A test with one or more comprehensive questions that require a detailed and comprehensive understanding of the course material, far beyond basic knowledge of facts. These exams challenge your knowledge and require you to put your answer in your own words. Essay writing will comprise a large amount of your college life.

Management
Time Management- there are 168 hours in a week. A developed process of creating a balance between academics and social responsibilities. How you utilize them will determine your academic success.

Incomplete Grade
A temporary grade that faculty can award a passing student who, for reasons outside his or her control (illness, death in the family, etc.) cannot complete all coursework and assignments in each term. Students typically have one semester following the incomplete to meet with the professor and complete the work.

Commit
Complete all assignments and take the college journey one semester at a time.

Study-time
Schedule time allotted for every hour in class, students should be studying two (2) to three (3) hours.

Undecided Student
A student who enters college with an undeclared major. Colleges often offer special programs for undecided students with names such as Discovery Students or StudentExplorers. These students are often put into programs to assist them in finding their majors, thereis no need to rush in choosing a major—at least until the end of the sophomore year.

Class Participation
Being presently present, asking questions, and participating in class discussions. Some faculty members grade class participation or reward bonus points. To get themost out of any class it is best to not only attend but participate in class discussions.

Cornell Note-Taking Method
A note-taking method used during class lectures; includes five (5) Rs Record, Reduce, Recite, Reflect, and Review.

Elective Courses
Additional courses outside of your major courses, which make up about half of the credits for degree completion (associate or bachelors). They are also an opportunity to expand your interests and learning.

Study Methods
Tools that aid students in developing effective long-term strategies. Strategies that help students not only study but become applicable and practical tools. Some common studymethods include SQ3R, Mnemonics, Mind-mapping, and ASPIRE.

Syllabus
A contract between the student and instructor, which contains the requirements for thecourse.

Secondary Research Sources
Published writings and reports that analyze, critique, or reporton a primary source and can be found in periodicals and reference books.

Kinesthetic/Tactile Learner
students who prefer to take in information through movement, manipulation, and touch. They tend to be able to operate equipment without reading instructions. They can easily learn dance steps and athletic maneuvers. About 5 percent of learners are kinesthetic/tactile.

Independent Study
A specialized course of study under the supervision of a faculty member. The topic is mutually agreed upon between the student and supervising faculty member. The burden is usually on the student to conduct a much more self-directed study plan than in a normal class setting.

Lecture
A class session in which the instructor speaks on a specific topic or topics for the entire class period. A very common method of college instruction, lectures require a strong note-taking strategy.

Life-Balance
Perhaps one of the most important things for academic success is finding a balance among all the demands college students face. Some of the best students are those who are very involved in social and professional activities on campus, but being too involved can alsoaffect your ability to study.

Study Schedule
Studying in college is best done by regularly reviewing course material in smaller chunks—to help train your brain into thinking and retaining information differently and avoiding all-night cramming for an upcoming test or assignment, and giving you a more positiveattitude about learning. Professors recommend two to three hours of out-of-class study time for each hour of class time.

CORNELL NOTE-TAKING METHOD
(IN CLASS NOTE-TAKING)

Taking notes is an important part of academic success in college. The Cornell Note-Taking Method is used to note important information heard while in class listening to lectures, etc. This method helps students to organize their thoughts along with the professor's lecture or ideas written on the screen or board. This method created by Professor Walter Pauk consists of three parts cue, notes area, and summary, which can also be broken down into five Rs: Record, Reduce, Recite, Reflect, Review.

APPLICATION

Use an 8.5 by 11 sheet of paper and divide it into three parts see image at right.

Cue- This section is used for key words heard during the lecture. These words will be easy to recall and review as vocabulary.

Note area- The heart of the system. Students should not attempt to transcribe verbatim every word spoken by the instructor. Separate the essential and the non-essential material. Generally, if it is on the board, it is probably important enough to include in your notes. Develop a system of abbreviations you understand. Use these to write in telegraphic sentences, which include only enough words to carry the essential meaning. Shorthand that is often used in text messages can also be used here.

Summaries- A summary is brief—at most, only a few sentences. The page summary provides a concise review of the important material on the page. More importantly, the summary forces the student to view the material in a way that allows them to see how it all fits together. The summary should be written in your own words, which helps you to own the information.

SQ3R METHOD
(TEXTBOOK NOTE-TAKING)

The SQ3R Method is a reading comprehension five-step system used while taking notes when reading a textbook. The system is designed to have the students go over the material more thanonce, which aids in greater comprehension and retaining the information for later purposes, classes discussion, exams, etc. The components of the SQ3R method are Survey, Question, Read, Recite, Review.

1. **Survey:** This simply means to scan the written material. This quick review should reveal the general content and structure of the concepts. Scan the headings, subheadings, topic sentences of paragraphs, graphics, and pictures. This will provide a clear overview of the information to be covered.

2. **Question:** Develop questions concerning what the materials are about. As the learner scansthe material, generate questions to be answered later by careful reading.

3. **Read:** Read all the material carefully and look for the answers to the questions that were developed. Learners should take notes as they read the material, which expands the concepts andanswers to the questions.

4. **Recite:** Learners should rephrase notes into their own words as is done in the five R's method.

5. **Review:** Again, as in the five R's, learners should periodically review their notes to keep theinformation fresh in their minds.

SURVEY	Survey the entire chapter by scanning the titles, headings, pictures and chapter summaries to obtain a general understanding of the concept.
QUESTION	As you survey, actively ask yourself questions about the information in the various sections.
READ	Actively read for comprehension to locate the concepts and facts.
RECITE	Transfer information to long-term memory by answering the questions in your own words.
REVIEW	Practice and rehearse the main ideas/concepts then reflect on key learning concepts

Again, there are many study methods, and this method is only one of many. We offer it to add to your toolbox

READING STRATEGIES

Regardless of the subject matter, students who utilize a reading strategy (and there's more than one) have a greater level of comprehension, can read a larger quantity of materials, and apply the material to discussions or research papers. Below is a picture outline of a reading strategy, read across not up and down.

Locate Key Words	Make Predictions	Use Word Attack Strategies re-read-ing Prefix Root Suffix
Visualize	Use Graphic Organizers (MAIN IDEA)	Evaluate Understanding
Re-read the Text	Activate Prior Knowledge	Use Context Clues
Infer Meaning READ (between the lines)	Think Aloud--Talk It out	Summarize the Story Using its Key Elements Characters ↳Setting ↳Problem ↳Solution

Adapted from https://www.teachthought.com/literacy/25-reading-strategies-that-work-in-every-content-area/

TIME MANAGEMENT

There are several things to help students be successful in college and time management is one of them. Time Management is simply put as a process, set of skills, tools or systems, to help you be more productive and efficient. In addition to utilizing your smartphone calendar for appointments, and assignment due-date reminders; the S.M.A.R.T system is very helpful not just for college but life. The goal as a college student is to work smart and not hard. This can be accomplished in various ways, however, utilizing the S.M.A.R.T systems for time management means:

Specific- Begin with an action plan! Be clear and detailed. Writing everything down helps to create a clear path of what needs to be done, by when, and why is this important. Have specific goals (assignments/activities) laid out each day. Create a specific process through which you intend to get each one of them accomplished.

Measurable- Every important aspect of your life requires a measure of time. There are several areas that relate to each. Know that not everything can fit in one day. Manage smaller things first. Keep track of your progress; it helps to keep you motivated.

Achievable- Organizing your schedule will highlight what you can accomplish with a specific timeframe successfully. Do not try to juggle several things at the same time or shift back and forth between tasks. Instead, implement the principle of itemizing and prioritizing.

Realistic- It's easy to get overwhelmed by large projects and big exams, especially when students pack their schedules with unrealistic expectations to complete and or participate in numerous activities in a short period of time, thus leading to anxiety and possibly procrastination. Start with shorter, simpler to-do items and then move on to larger projects or assignments.

Time-bound- Tangible with a Target Date – You will be able to manage time more effectively when you put clear benchmarks (due dates) in place as a completion goal. A goal is tangible when you can experience it with one of the senses, that is, taste, touch, smell, sight, or hearing. When your goal is tangible, you have a better chance of making it specific and measurable, and thus attainable.

Managing your time will help you get a better idea of how much time you need to prepare for each subject. **We all get 168 hours a week.** How effectively you manage your time will determine how successful you will not only be in college but in life.

TIME MANAGEMENT SELF-ASSESSMENT

		Never	Seldom	Often	Always
1.	I use a day planner or a student planner.				
2.	I schedule tests and assignments on a monthly calendar.				
3.	I am able to prioritize my tasks.				
4.	My assignments are handed in on time.				
5.	I attend class on a regular basis.				
6.	I have enough time to do daily homework assignments and reading.				
7.	I have enough time to study for tests.				
8.	I am able to balance other time commitments (sports, friends, family, work) with school.				
9.	I keep track of my grades in each class.				
10.	I do things right when they are assigned instead of putting them off.				
11.	I am able to sit down and do work for one hour without being distracted.				
12.	I break larger tasks down into more manageable parts.				
	TOTAL				

If your total is more than 6 in the Never or Seldom columns, consider reassessing how you utilize your time.

QUICK TIP:
HOW TO BREAK DOWN YOUR SEMESTER

SCHEDULES

SEMESTER SCHEDULE	WEEKLY SCHEDULE	DAILY TO-DO LIST
Create a 4 month calendar for the semester	Create a 7 day, 24 hour schedule	Use a daytimer for daily to-do lists (avoid loose scraps of paper)
Write in all assignment deadlines, tests and exams	Put in all classes, work hours & other appointments or events	Each day, make a list of all the tasks you need to do
Fill in your work schedule as far ahead as you can	Highlight all times that are marked. The remaining hours can be filled	Prioritize each task as (A) high, (B) medium or (C) low priority
Include all holidays	Using the semester schedule, mark time to prepare for tests / deadlines	Start with the high priority tasks
Add in other commitments or events you need to plan around	Allow time for daily homework and reading assignments	As you complete each task, cross it off the list
	Mark in time to review notes within 24 hours of the class	Unfinished tasks can be moved to the next day's list

When you fail to plan, you plan to fail. Don't let that be your story!

STUDY STRATEGIES

No two people study the same way, and there is little doubt that what works for one person may not work for another. However, there are some general techniques that seem to produce good results. No one would argue that every subject that you have to take is going to be so interesting that studying it is not work but a pleasure. We can only wish! Everyone is different, and for some students, studying and being motivated to learn comes naturally. If not don't despair, there is hope! Your success in high school and college is dependent on your ability to study effectively and efficiently. **There is no magic formula for success in preparing for tests or written or oral assignments.** Studying any material requires work!

Active studying includes, but is not limited to the following.

- Create study guides by topic. Formulate questions and problems and write out complete answers. Create your own quiz
- Say the information aloud in your own words as if you are the instructor and teaching the concepts to a class
- Develop examples that relate to your own experiences
- Create mind-mapping diagrams that explain the material you are studying
- For non-technical classes (e.g., English, History, Psychology), figure out the big ideas so you can explain, contrast, and re-evaluate them
- For technical classes, work through the problems and explain each of the steps and why they work
- Study in terms of the question, evidence, and conclusion:

    o What is the question posed by the instructor or author?

    o What is the evidence that they present?

    o What is the conclusion?

STUDY STRATEGIES (CONTINUED)

UNDERSTANDING YOUR STUDY CYCLE

A study cycle developed by Frank Christ may vary for each person. However, understanding the cycle helps break down the different parts of studying.

- **Previewing-** before class
- **Attending class-** actively taking notes
- **Reviewing-** fill in the missing holes from the notes taken in class
- **Study-** in short, intense increments 30-45 minutes and or within 30-60 minutes of eating
- **Checking your understanding-** develop a practice self-test or discuss what you learned with classmates
- **Silence & Setting-** Find the best place where you can study and not be disturbed. A change in environment has been known to help. Silence and setting are your friends!
- **Time-** Having time to study is vital, equally as important is understanding the best time of day for you to study
- **Downtime-** an opportunity to catch up on assignments, reading, and or to stay ahead Don't let downtime get you left behind.

Although each step may seem obvious at a glance, all too often students try to take shortcuts and miss opportunities for good learning.

Adapted from www. Prepexpert.com, 2021

TEST TAKING AND STUDY STRATEGIES SELF-ASSESSMENT

		Never	Seldom	Often	Always
1.	I have a study routine.				
2.	I study for tests in a comfortable, distraction free place.				
3.	I review my notes within 12-24 hours of class.				
4.	I do weekly reviews of both class and textbook material.				
5.	I quiz myself when I study.				
6.	I develop study questions from class and text material and use these questions for studying.				
7.	I study in groups with other classmates.				
8.	I use cue cards as a study tool.				
9.	I use mind-mapping as a study tool.				
10.	On tests/exams, I do well on multiple choice questions.				
11.	On tests/exams, I do well on short answer questions.				
12.	On tests/exams, I do well on essay questions.				
	TOTAL				

If your total is more than 6 in the Never or Seldom columns, consider reassessing your study strategies.

TEST TAKING

Test-taking is a BIG part of college life and can be nerve-wracking and create anxiety. The purpose of test-taking is to evaluate the level of understanding of acquired information from classroom lecturers and outside readings. Below are a few strategies to assist you with the various types of tests you might encounter.

Keep in mind the importance of preparing yourself physically, mentally and emotionally before each of your tests and exams.

WHEN THE TEST IS IN YOUR HANDS

- **Read** over the **entire test** before you begin.

- When reading each question consider the FACTS.

F	What **form** should your answer take?
A	What **aids** can you use - calculator, formulas, books...?
C	Do you have any **choice** or do you need to do all of the questions?
T	How much **time** can you allow for each question?
S	How will you be **scored** on each question? How much is each question worth?

- Jot down any key words or ideas that come to mind when you are reading through the test.

- Underline or highlight **key words** in the questions. These words may include rate, list, describe, outline, argue, criticize, compare, contrast and so on.

- If there is choice in how many or which questions to do, note to yourself which one(s) you want to omit.

- Consider how much time you intend to spend on each question while still allowing 5 to 10 minutes to **check your work**.

- First complete questions you can answer, starting with those worth the most marks. If you have time, tackle the ones you are not sure you can do, beginning with those worth the most marks.

TEST TAKING TIPS FOR DIFFERENT EXAM QUESTIONS

True & false tips

- Usually there are more true answers than false on most test
- If there is no guessing penalty you have a 50% chance of getting the answer right
- Qualifiers like always, never and every mean the statement must be true all the time
- If any part of the question is false, then the entire statement is false, but because part of the statement is true doesn't mean the entire statement is true

Multiple-choice tips

- Read the question before you look at the answers
- Come up with an answer before you look at the choices
- Eliminate answers you know aren't right
- Read all answers before choosing
- If there is no penalty for guessing take an educated guess using the process of elimination
- In questions with an "all of the above" choice if at least two of the choices are true then all of the above is probably the answer
- In questions with an "all of the above" & "none of the above" choice if you are certain that at least one statement is true don't choose none of the above or one of the statements are false don't choose all of the above
- Usually the correct answer is the choice with the most information

Short answer tips

- Use flashcards, write key terms, dates, and concepts on the front with definitions and explanations on the back
- Try not to leave an answer blank
- Read the question carefully and make sure that you answer everything that it asks for, some short answers have multiple parts
- Try to anticipate the questions that will be asked on the test and prepare for them. Usually what the instructor emphasizes in class will be on the test

TEST TAKING TIPS FOR DIFFERENT EXAM QUESTIONS (CONTINUED)

Essay tips
- Read the question carefully
- Make sure you understand that the question is asking you, if not ask the instructor
- Budget your time, don't spend the entire test time on one essay
- If the questions ask for facts don't give a personal opinion on the topic
- When writing, be as neat as possible, if an instructor has to attempt to figure out what you are trying to convey you will lose substance to your essay and subsequently lose points
- If you have time proofread
- Stick to the main idea of the topic

Math test tips
- Repetition is important in Math; you will learn how to solve them by doing them so keep practicing
- Work on practice problems for each topic ranging in levels of difficulty
- When you get your exam, write down all key formula on the margin of your paper so you don't forget them in the middle of the exam, use it as a reference page
- Show all your work (especially when partial credit is being awarded) and write as legible as possible
- When practicing, try to solve a problem on your own first then look at the answer or seek help if you are having trouble
- Check over your test after you are done with it. Look for careless mistakes such as making sure the decimal is in the right place; make sure you read all the directions correctly, that you have put a negative sign if needed

Reducing your test anxiety
- Being well prepared for the test is the best way to reduce test-taking anxiety
- Space out your study over a few days or weeks to continually review class material. DO NOT wait until the night before to cram
- Try to maintain a positive attitude while preparing for the test and during the test
- Exercising a few days before the test will help reduce stress

- Good night's sleep before the test
- Show up to class early so you won't have to worry about being late
- Skim through the test so that you have a good idea of how to pace yourself
- Write important formula, definitions, and keywords
- Do simple questions first to help build up your confidence
- Focus on the question at hand don't let your mind wonder
- Stay relaxed, if you are beginning to get nervous take a few deep breaths slowly to relax and then get back to work

INFORMATION LITERACY

According to the American Library Association, "Information literacy is a set of abilities requiring individuals to 'recognize when information is needed and have the ability to locate, evaluate, and use effectively the needed information."

In the below diagram, you will notice that to be truly 'information literate' requires that you simultaneously develop:

- Awareness of how you engage with the digital world
- How you find meaning in the information you discover
- How to articulate what kind of information you require
- How to use information ethically
- Understand the role you can play in the communication in your profession and
- How you evaluate the information for credibility and authority

INFORMATION LITERACY

(Diagram showing four quadrants around a central "INFORMATION LITERACY — critical thinking and evaluation" core:)

- **ACADEMIC LITERACIES** — learning development; study skills and academic writing
- **NEW LITERACIES** — multimodal learning; transliteracies
- **MEDIA LITERACY** — critical use of non-textual communication formats; critical analysis
- **DIGITAL LITERACY** — Ethics and E-Safety; computer literacy and functional skills; search skills

Coonan, E., & Jane, S. (2014, April 29). "My dolly's bigger than your dolly", or, Why our labels no longer matter. Retrieved April 29, 2016, from https://librariangoddess.wordpress.com/2014/04/29/my-dollys-bigger/

LEARNING STYLES

We all have preferred styles of learning. Every individual processes information and experienceinto knowledge better when the activity is best suited to their learning style. *A learning style is aconsistent way in which a person perceives, conceptualizes, organizes, and recalls information.* Students develop a personal learning style based on their culture, genetics, previous learning experiences, and surrounding society.

By matching teaching styles (methods) with learning styles, chances improve for successfullearning. Students master objectives with greater ease and less time, less boredom. Their relationship with the teacher often improves as does their self-esteem and enjoyment of the learning process.

THE STYLES

https://medium.com/@rgarza7/individual-learning-styles-and-learning-to-code-41eb8054453a

The awareness of learning styles for students is usually a direct result of the teaching styles students have been exposed to. Teaching styles and learning styles are like two sides of one coin. The work of Dr's R. Bandler, and J. Grinder, in the field of *Neuro-Linguistic Programming*, produced the following categories: **visual** (seeing), **auditory** (hearing), **kinesthetic** (moving) or (touching). Most students will be more drawn to one or two of these categories as a method of learning. That doesn't mean you will be unable to learn using other modalities, it just indicates your preferred method.

LEARNING STYLES (CONTINUED)

A visual style suggests
- Facial and body movements are important
- Viewing posters, images, and graphics help increase understanding
- Often recognize words by sight & shape
- Prefer lists and boxes/tables to organize thoughts
- Recall information by remembering how it was set out on a page

An auditory style suggests
- Verbal (listening) instructions are the primary way of comprehending
- A preference for dialogue, discussions, and podcasts etc.
- Problems are analyzed/solved by talking about them
- Spoken rhythms and sounds (tone) act as a memory aid

A verbal style suggests
- An enjoyment for language, reading, and writing
- Using mnemonic devices, acronyms, diagrams

A kinesthetic/tactile style suggests
- Action is important; the need to "do something" as a key part of instruction or learning
- Sitting still for long periods is hard
- Using movement as a memory aid
- Writing/notes and drawing are key elements in processing and remembering
- Hands-on activities like projects and demonstrations are preferred

A logical-Mathematical style suggests
- The capacity to conceptualize the logical relations among actions orsymbols (e.g. mathematicians, scientists)
- Running simulation-type games, working through word problems, understanding cause and effects, and code stimulates learning

A social (interpersonal) style suggests
- Enjoyment while working in groups (study groups)
- The ability to interact effectively with others, Sensitivity to others' moods and feelings

A solitary (intrapersonal) style suggests
- Silence is your friend. A great need for quiet time alone to best process information

The idea behind multiple learning styles is to highlight that students learn more than one way, and they can demonstrate their knowledge and abilities in different ways. Note, a students' learning style or preference can change depending on the subject matter, be flexible.

CRITICAL THINKING

Critical thinking involves questioning established ideas, creating new ideas, and using information to solve and or support problems. In part critical thinking allows one to deconstruct a situation to reveal its bias and manipulation. Part of obtaining a college degree is to develop and exercise this skill to think, speak, and write critically. The concept can be difficult to grasp because it requires students to set aside assumptions and beliefs to think *without bias or judgment*. That is difficult to do! Critical thinking involves suspending your beliefs to explore and question topics from a "blank page" point of view. It also involves the ability to know facts from opinion when exploring a topic.

Benjamin Bloom was among the first to codify the idea of "lower" and "higher" thinking skills. First developed in the 1950s, Bloom's Taxonomy is still widely recognized by educators today. In this framework, skills are thought to build upon each other, starting with the most basic skills (recall and comprehension), progressing through more complex skills (application and analysis), and culminating with higher-order thinking skills (**HOTS**) such as synthesis, evaluation, and creation. The pyramid has been revised over the years, but the basic idea remains the same.

BLOOM'S TAXONOMY

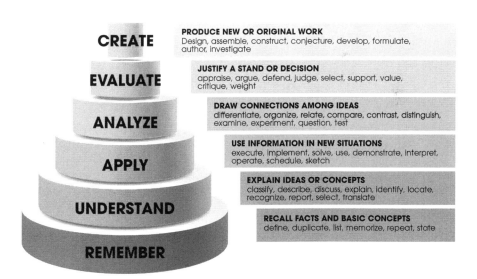

CRITICAL THINKING TIPS

Have an open mindset (thought process). A mindset is a set of thoughts developed over time based on experiences, environment and culture. However, these experiences are NOT the only experiences to address a situation. When a new situation arises be prepared to shift your mindset.

Tolerance for others' ideas. Be open to exchange views from people of different backgrounds, cultures, experiences. Approach each situation with the thought to understand and not always to be understood.

Keep emotions in check. Our thoughts and values are important to us. Keeping emotions in check allows us to receive information in a clear manner and not let biases cloud the outcome.

Questions, Questions, & More Questions. Do not make it a practice to take information as reliable without posing some questions. Question the answer, question assumptions, and let WHY become a big part of your vocabulary.

Fact-finding. Gather as much information as you can. Information gathering allows you to weigh your options and make the most informed decision.

Analyze failures and mistakes. Learn from the mistake and lean into the lesson. Think how you can avoid making the same mistake next time.

Consider the pros and cons. Not all situations are black and white or straightforward. Examine all information to make an educated decision.

CRITICAL THINKING SELF-ASSESSMENT

		Never	Seldom	Often	Always
1.	I have a study routine.				
2.	I study for tests in a comfortable, distraction free place.				
3.	I review my notes within 12-24 hours of class.				
4.	I do weekly reviews of both class and textbook material.				
5.	I quiz myself when I study.				
6.	I develop study questions from class and text material and use these questions for studying.				
7.	I study in groups with other classmates.				
8.	I use cue cards as a study tool.				
9.	I use mind-mapping as a study tool.				
10.	On tests/exams, I do well on multiple choice questions.				
11.	On tests/exams, I do well on short answer questions.				
12.	On tests/exams, I do well on essay questions.				
	TOTAL				

If your total is more than 6 in the Never or Seldom columns, consider reassessing your criticalthinking strategies.

EMOTIONAL WELL-BEING

College students' mental health has always been a major concern across college campuses nationwide. Recently, there has been an alarming increase of mental health challenges among college students and has been compounded with a global pandemic - Covid-19. In a report issued by the American Council on Education (May, 2020) students from various backgrounds, ages, demographics reported higher levels of uncertainty and great amounts of stress dealing with their academics. Students who struggle with their emotional well-being, often have lower GPAs and disenroll from their studies. A study published in Frontier in Psychology (2021, V.6) females reported worse emotional well-being than males; and BIPOC students reported higher levels of stress than their white counterparts. Thus, highlighting the necessity for students and college campuses to engage in emotional well-being activities.

EMOTIONAL WELLNESS ACTIVITIES

Be positive. Sad emotions are a part of life, however, do not let them weigh you down and keep you stuck. A few things to jumpstart a positive mindset:

- Find something you did well every day
- Be kind to yourself and others— forgive yourself and others. Learn from the mistake, lean into the lesson
- Surround yourself with positive, healthy people
- Explore your beliefs about the meaning and purpose of life and use them to guide your decisions. Explore new experiences

Connect & Communicate. Research has shown that social communication and connections can have a powerful effect on our emotional and physical health. Connect and communicate by joining a club and expanding your circle. Also, don't hide behind social media. Here are a few other suggestions.

- Expand your horizons and join a virtual group focused on one of your favorite hobbies.
- Learn something new.
- Community involvement on or off-campus.

Stress buster. Stress is normal, eustress is good stress, however, too much distress drains your energy and makes it difficult to concentrate. Here are some healthy ways to cope with stress and boost your resilience.

- Get enough sleep
- Just 30 minutes a day of walking can boost your mood and reduce stress, increase those "feel-good hormones" endorphins
- Set priorities by deciding what must get done and what can wait. Do not overload yourself, say NO, when necessary. Acknowledge what you did accomplish.

- Mindfulness, meditation, yoga or tai chi may help you relax
- Talk with a mental health professional if you feel unable to cope, have suicidal thoughts, or use drugs or alcohol to cope

Quality sleep. It may be difficult to get the recommended 8-hours of sleep while in college, however, make the most of the hours you do sleep:

- Go to bed at the same time each night and get up at the same time each morning
- Sleep in a dark, quiet, comfortable environment
- Relax and limit the use of electronics an hour before bed
- Avoid alcohol and stimulants such as caffeine late in the day

Establish boundaries. Let NO be your friend! You cannot successfully be all things to all people. Some important ways to establish boundaries include:

- People will know how to treat and respect you once you let them know what you will and will not tolerate
- Don't feel like you need to say yes to avoid hurting someone's feelings
- Think of your ROR- Rate of Return of your time and energy versus the impact it will have
- Don't let people talk you into things you don't want to do or out of things you want to do

Be mindful. Mindfulness is about being completely aware of what's happening in the present. It means not living your life on "autopilot." To be more mindful:

- Take a moment, think and breathe before responding to requests.
- Be present in each moment, conversations, eating. What is being said, the food you are eating, i.e., tastes, smells, etc.
- Participate in campus wellness programs such as yoga and meditation classes, stress-reduction programs, and or read books.

Cope with loss. Loss is part of the cycle of life. The death of a loved one and even a job can feel overwhelming. Having supportive family and friends helps during the process. Some coping strategies:

- It's OK to put yourself first. Rest, eat right, exercise, and get enough sleep.
- Talk to caring friends or find a support group.
- Wait a while before making big decisions like moving or changing jobs.
- Talk with your doctor if you're having trouble with everyday activities.
- Mourning takes time. It's common to have roller-coaster emotions for a while.

EMOTIONAL WELL-BEING (CONTINUED)

Accept yourself. You are unique and wonderfully designed to do greatness. Self-sabotage gets you nowhere FAST! Love you and others will too. Steps to a happier you:

- Declare positive I AM affirmations to yourself daily.
- It is not about perfection it is about progress, give yourself grace.
- Don't assume; ask for clarity!
- You are an overcomer; it is often not as bad as you think.
- Failure is a step on the road to success, trust the process, trust yourself.

Ask for help. If you are suffering from emotional distress, it's OK to ask others for help. Everyone has moments of stress, and you are not alone. People to talk to include:

- A friend or family member you trust and who'll be a good listener is a good place to start.
- Get the perspective of others to hear how they would handle a situation.
- Seek the advice of a mental health professional, counselor, advisor, or wellness center professional.

FINANCIAL LITERACY

Enjoying the college experience is not cheap. The rising cost of college education has been the topic of discussion for decades. However, not having an awareness of financial literacy can make the experience even more expensive. Financial literacy is more than just acquiring information; it is about applying the information to your everyday life. Financial literacy is so important in a college student's life that Congress set up the Financial Literacy and Education Commission under the Fair and Accurate Credit Transaction Act in 2003.

To help you with gaining financial literacy, check out the *Six Money Mishaps and How to Get Back on Track*.

6 MONEY MISHAPS AND HOW TO GET YOUR MONEY BACK ON TRACK!

1. The To-Die For Credit Card Offer

You are checking out at your favorite store when the cashier mentions a special offer; store cardholders get 40% off. What a deal! You sign up for the card—and add a few more shirts that you were eyeing to your pile.

Reality Check: While the perks of the store card may seem like a no-brainer, these special credit cards often come with super-high interest rates and fees if you do not pay on time.

Get Back on Track: Set a rule that you will not open any credit cards while out shopping; it will help keep you from too-good-to-be-true offers. Research cards beforehand

2. The Sky-High Cell Phone Bill

You signed up for the plan that is supposed to be $39.95 a month. So, when you get the bill for three times that amount, you are in shock!

Reality Check: Lots of things can increase your cell phone bill. Going over minutes, text msg, game purchases.

Get back on track: Find out the real cost associated with your cell phone i.e., taxes. Compare plans, adjust your plan according to your usage.

3. The Split Check Disaster

You let your BFF pick the homecoming restaurant and surprise, the menu carries an expensive price tag. You keep your menu choice simple with a salad, but the bill arrives, and the suggestion is to split the check equally.

Reality Check: Friends and financial issues often do not mix (especially without a conversation ahead of time). Do not feel pressured to pay for something you did not indulge in.

Speaking up can save you a lot of headaches in the future.

Get Back on Track: Tell your friends what your financial constraints are, honesty helps.

4. The Barely There Paycheck

You're excited about your first job while in college, not so excited about the wait for your first paycheck. And then you get it and there are a lot more entities that got to it first—OMG all the deductions.

Reality Check: You always will bring home less than what they told you in the interview. Taxes, social security, healthcare etc.

Get Back on Track: Learn the difference between gross and net income, even for those PT jobs. Understanding what tax bracket you fall into, will help you understand why the IRS takes their share first

5. The Lunchtime Dilemma

There is an excitement with grabbing lunch or dinner off-campus with friends, however, the extra cost in transportation—gas, plus food and extra treats like dessert can add up.

Reality Check: Small purchases can have a major financial impact. A Starbucks coffee at $4 Mon-Fri equals $100 for the month. And to think you did not even buy anything to eat.

Get Back on Track: Decide on a budget, stick to it. If you blow your budget, try making lunch or utilize your meal plan more.

6. The Rotating Saving

Homecoming is approaching and you have your eye on a new outfit. Your credit cards are maxed out, so you take all that is left in your savings account. Your funds are low but you're looking good for homecoming.

Reality Check: Dipping into your savings for extracurricular activities will leave you with no finances in case of emergencies.

Get Back on Track: Open two accounts, one where you pay yourself first, automatic payments, and don't touch it. Second, stay within your budget. Cut your spending habits. Track spending vs savings.

Adapted from: http://www.weareteachers.com

Notes

Notes

Notes

Notes

Notes

Made in the USA
Middletown, DE
28 September 2023